THE SHABUNIN AFFAIR

Also by Walter Kerr:

The Russian Army
The Secret of Stalingrad

The Shabunin Affair

*An Episode in the Life
of Leo Tolstoy*

Walter Kerr

Cornell University Press

<small>Ithaca and London</small>

First published in 1982 by Cornell University Press.
Published in the United Kingdom by Cornell University Press Ltd.,
Ely House, 37 Dover Street, London W1X 4HQ.

Excerpts from *Anna Karenina* by Leo Tolstoy, translated by David Magarshack, copyright © 1961 by David Magarshack, are reprinted by arrangement with the New American Library, Inc., New York, New York.

International Standard Book Number 0-8014-1461-X
Library of Congress Catalog Card Number 81-70715
Printed in the United States of America
*Librarians: Library of Congress cataloging information
appears on the last page of the book.*

The paper in this book is acid-free, and meets the guidelines for permanence and durability of the Committee on Production Guidelines for Book Longevity of the Council on Library Resources.

To Vivianne, to Cynthia, to Philip, and to Helen
—as always

Contents

Contents

Preface

This is the story of a strange and terrible incident that had strange and terrible consequences. It is about Leo Tolstoy's appearance as counsel for the defense at the court-martial of a soldier who faced death by firing squad and how what happened at that time, when Tolstoy was thirty-seven years old and writing *War and Peace*, affected his life and work. So far as I know, the story has not been told before, except briefly, incompletely—in part because Tolstoy, out of feelings of guilt and remorse, rarely wrote or spoke of the affair, in part because the army file on the matter has been buried until now in the military-historical archives in Moscow. There is monstrous irony here. Tolstoy believed—and died believing—that he bore some responsibility for the outcome of the case; but the Moscow file that will be published for the first time in these pages shows him to have been the unsuspecting victim of chilling intrigue in the upper reaches of the army. In a little-known letter written forty-two years after the event, he said the entire affair had had much more influence on his life than the loss of or recovery of his wealth or literary success or failure or the death of loved ones.[1]

Now, one may believe this was an overstatement—Tolstoy was given to exaggeration—but the puzzling crisis that overcame him when, after *Anna Karenina*, he stopped writing novels, and much of what he wrote after that—against capital punishment, against violence in any form, against church and state and the instruments of church and state—indicate it was indeed a shattering experience. This is understandable. The death penalty affects anyone who has any connection with it, and Tolstoy's connection with the Shabunin affair was direct, so disconcerting, so disturbing when he came to reflect upon it, that the way he handled it and its aftermath brings an added measure of understanding to the character of this complicated man. It suggests he was neither a saint, as some of his contemporaries believed, nor a hypocritical crank, as others evidently thought, but an intensely private, intensely human being who suffered painfully and alone in the manner of all intensely private, intensely human beings. Tolstoy warred against capital punishment until a few days before his death in 1910; but from 1866, when the incident occurred, until 1908 he revealed little of what he knew of the affair, and even then he withheld details he could not bring himself to disclose. In all his known diaries and diary notes, he referred to the case only three times, hastily, cryptically. In the 8,500 or more of his letters that survive, he mentioned it in only five. He did not allude to it in the outline of his life that he sent to Pavel Biryukov, his friend and Russian biographer, before Biryukov sat down to write, and he threw Aylmer Maude, his friend and English biographer, off the scent by telling Maude in reply to a question that of the four occasions when he had spoken in public, the time he had done so with the most assurance and satisfaction to himself was at Shabunin's trial.[2]

But the day came when Tolstoy faced questions he could not or would not evade. It was early 1908, and Biryukov was gathering material for his third volume (the first was out, the second at the printer's) when to his astonishment and horror he came across a file that shook him to the depths of his soul. He had known Tolstoy for twenty-four years, been an intimate friend, stayed at his house, been one of his disciples, courted one of his daughters, served as his secretary, managed his publishing enterprise, suffered exile on Tolstoy's account, and he had never heard of the case. What about it? he asked. Was it true? And Tolstoy broke down. Yes, he said (for so he wrongly thought), it all had happened as the clippings, notes, and other papers indicated. Weeks later he wrote a letter, intended for publication, recalling the affair. Nikolai Gusev, Tolstoy's secretary, says in his diary that Tolstoy burst into tears three times in the course of the dictation.[3] Well he might have. The Shabunin affair was his secret cross, and he was telling all, or as much as he knew and was prepared to tell, whatever embarrassment it might cause him, however humiliating it might be to expose at long last his innermost thoughts and feelings.

Oddly enough, to little avail. Biryukov hastily inserted in his second volume a chapter that included the text of the letter, but the inferential data suggest that members of Tolstoy's family rallied round to protect Tolstoy from himself and his new-found candor. In the available part of the diary and memoirs of his wife, Sonya, and in the memoirs of their five children who published their recollections, the letter is ignored, the case scarcely referred to. Sonya gives it a paragraph, son Ilya another, daughter Alexandra four paragraphs, son Sergei nothing, son Leo nothing, daughter Tatyana nothing, and neither the letter nor the case is mentioned in the memoirs of Tolstoy's favorite sister-in-law, Tanya—Sonya's sister, the model for Natasha in *War and Peace*—who passed much of the summer of 1866 with the Tolstoys and knew almost everyone involved. It is then not surprising that Tolstoy's biographers, except for Biryukov and to a lesser extent Gusev, dispose of the matter briefly when they write of it at all. Henri Troyat gives it three and a half pages (though he says Tolstoy was "thoroughly demoralized" by the affair),[4] Ernest J. Simmons about two (but he makes the point that this was an experience Tolstoy "always remembered with chagrin and self-condemnation"),[5] Maude about three, Nathan Haskell Dole two, George Rapall Noyes one, Edward Steiner nothing, Romain Rolland nothing, Alexander Nazaroff nothing, Derrick Leon nothing. Not one of them, not even Biryukov or Gusev, draws attention to Tolstoy's long silence or supports or questions his judgment of the affair.

I would not like to be misunderstood here. To write a biography of Tolstoy is an overwhelming task, and the work of several of these men, especially Simmons and Troyat, may never be surpassed. Nor do I mean to imply that this case alone shaped Tolstoy's life and work or alone was responsible for the spiritual crisis that overcame him in late middle age. He was affected strongly by many circumstances and character traits: by an aristocratic background, his service as a soldier in the Caucasus and in the Crimean war, an early dissolute life, a troubled conscience, love of country life and contempt for St. Petersburg and Moscow society, repression under four emperors (Nicholas I, Alexander II, Alexander III, and Nicholas II), the severe lot of the peasants (which was improved, but not drastically, by the emancipation of the serfs in 1861), an impulse to religion that was combined with an opposition to church dogma his reason could not accept, a tendency to reject conventional thought, stubborn questions about the meaning of life, fear of death, and so on. But we are dealing with an appalling sequence of events from which there emerges a portrait of the man and artist as he developed from the days of *War and Peace* through *Anna Karenina* to *Resurrection*. It is a portrait that shows more suffering about the eyes than is commonly imagined.

WALTER KERR

Santa Fe, New Mexico

Author's Notes

The Moscow file on the Shabunin affair consists of ten handwritten documents, of which three are of a purely administrative nature and seven go to the heart of the matter. I wish to express here my thanks to the Information Department of the Soviet Embassy in Washington and the Novosti Press Agency in Moscow, which sought them out and located them for me after a search of many months. The documents are of considerable historical interest and, incidentally, clarify a doubt that has long existed about the spelling of the last name of the soldier who had such a lasting effect on Tolstoy's life. In the ninety volumes of Tolstoy's *Complete Works* the name is written *Shibunin* (most frequently), *Shebunin* (occasionally), and *Shabunin* (rarely).[1] The documents consistently spell it *Shabunin*. They also support the contention of Nikolai Gusev, Tolstoy's secretary, that General Dmitri Milyutin, the minister of war, and Alexander II were involved in the case early on.[2]

I also am indebted to the editors of the *Complete Works* for their scholarly footnotes and to Gusev, who, although he did not have access to the Moscow file, revealed its existence. Other sources whose works have been helpful are Pavel Biryukov, Tolstoy's official biographer; other biographers, among them Ernest J. Simmons, Henri Troyat, and

13

Author's Notes

Aylmer Maude; R. F. Christian, who has translated many of Tolstoy's letters; and several translators of his best-known works, including Maude and his wife, Louise (*War and Peace*), David Magarshack (*Anna Karenina*), Nathan Haskell Dole (*Confession*), and Vera Traill (*Resurrection*). Another useful source was the August 24, 1903, issue of *Pravo*, a St. Petersburg legal journal, whose report on the affair was based on a contemporary account. Finally, I owe a special debt to Michael Ossorgin, of St. John's College in Santa Fe, New Mexico, who reviewed and made many valuable suggestions about my own translations from the Russian, among them Tolstoy's plea to the court in 1866, his letter to Biryukov in 1908, and his rare but telling references to the case in the years between. Professor Ossorgin is not only a scholar with an intense interest in Russian literature, but one with an unusual knowledge of the life and works of Tolstoy, to whose family he is related. He was particularly helpful to me when the time came to penetrate the mysteries of the handwritten documents in the Moscow file.

I am grateful to Macmillan Publishing Co., Inc., for permission to reprint passages from Tatyana A. Kuzminskaya's *Tolstoy as I Knew Him: My Life at Home and at Yasnaya Polyana*, copyright 1948 by American Council of Learned Societies; to Athlone Press and Charles Scribner's Sons for permission to reprint materials from *Tolstoy's Letters*, Selected, Edited, and Translated by R. F. Christian, © (copyright) 1978 by R. F. Christian (New York: Charles Scribner's Sons, 1978); to Oxford University Press for permission to quote from the English translation of *War and Peace* by Louise and Aylmer Maude; to Little, Brown and Company for permission to quote from *Leo Tolstoy* by Ernest J. Simmons, copyright 1945, 1946 by Ernest J. Simmons; to Hamish Hamilton Ltd. for permission to quote from *Resurrection* by Leo Tolstoy, translated by Vera Traill; and to Victor Gollancz Ltd. for permission to quote from *The Diary of Tolstoy's Wife, 1860–1891*, by Sonya A. Tolstoy, translated by Alexander Werth.

In general, I have followed the transliteration system recommended by the United States Board of Geographic Names, but one is tempted to be somewhat arbitrary about personal names because they are often something of a problem for English-speaking readers. Accordingly, except in quotations, titles, and the familiar Anna Karenina and Katusha Maslova, I have avoided the feminine endings of family names and dropped the customary patronymics. My preference is for such first names as Andrei, Nikolai, Sergei, and Vasili instead of Andrew, Nicholas, Sergius, and Basil. Exceptions are Leo (for Tolstoy, because that is how he wrote his name in English), Peter, Alexander, and Nicholas for the tsars (because they are so known), and, generally, Alexander for Aleksandr (because the one sounds reasonable, the other awkward).

All dates except that of Eugene Schuyler's birth are according to the Julian calendar, which was twelve days behind our Gregorian calendar in the nineteenth century, thirteen days in the twentieth.

Cast of Characters

Leo Tolstoy
Sofya (Sonya) Tolstoy, his wife
Tatyana (Tanya) Bers, Sonya's younger sister
Colonel Yunosha
Lieutenant Grigori Kolokoltsov
Ensign Alexander Stasyulevich } of the Sixty-fifth Moscow
Private Vasili Shabunin Infantry Regiment
Captain Yasevich, a Pole
Cadet Nikolai Ovsiannikov
Alexander Bibikov, Tolstoy's neighbor
Alexandra Tolstoy, Leo's first cousin once removed
General Gildenshtubbe, commander in chief of the Moscow
    Military District
General Dmitri Milyutin, minister of war
Tsar Alexander II
Afanasi Fet, poet and friend of Tolstoy
Dmitri Dyakov, landowner and friend of Tolstoy
Sergei Tolstoy, Leo's older brother
Marya Tolstoy, Leo's younger sister
Eugene Schuyler, American counsul in Moscow
Alexander Goldenweizer, pianist and friend of Tolstoy
Dushan Makovitsky, physician and friend of Tolstoy
Pavel Biryukov, friend and biographer
Aylmer Maude, friend and biographer
Nikolai Gusev, secretary and biographer

Also landowners, peasants, wanderers, priests, and shackled convicts, who in the summer of 1866 were building a rail line from Moscow to Tula and on past Tolstoy's estate at Yasnaya Polyana to Kiev.

PART ONE

Some Call It Murder

Russia and summer never do well together.
—Platon Karatayev in *War and Peace*

1

Tolstoy for the Defense

They all spoke of his eyes. "The most eloquent eyes I have ever seen," said Maxim Gorky; "a thousand eyes in one pair." "Oh, of course, his eyes," wrote Vladimir Nemirovich-Danchenko, playwright and stage designer; "those eagle eyes, the eyes of a kind and clever bird of prey."[1]

I think I see them now. They were gray and steady and glared from beneath overhanging brows, diverting attention from a nose that was a little too prominent and ears that were much too large, giving to an otherwise unengaging countenance an attractive appearance that was enhanced by chestnut hair and a full chestnut beard. At a later time the beard would be white and wispy, but in the summer of 1866, when he was thirty-seven years old, its color contributed to the overall impression of strength that was conveyed by a wiry body, a firm, determined mouth, and those quizzical, challenging eyes.

The impression was no illusion. Tolstoy was a fighter who made up his own mind and defended his opinions at every opportunity, conceding little to anyone about anything at any time. In short, he was a man to have on one's side in a crisis, which is one reason why in early July of that eventful year (the day is uncertain in the public record) two horsemen rode into the village of Yasnaya Polyana, in the Tula region, south of Moscow. They turned off the highway and, leaving the village with its thatched roofs behind them, passed between two low, round towers, painted white, which marked the entrance to Tolstoy's estate. I call it an estate but it was really an unproductive farm of some 2,400 acres and pretty much run down. The paint on the old brick towers was peeling. The tree-lined avenue leading to the sheds and barns was unswept. Beyond the sheds and barns, which had need of repair, were two small stone houses, one to the left, the other to the right. Between the houses, which were detached wings of the old family mansion, there was a gaping hole in the ground, choked with untamed weeds and mushrooming saplings, where the mansion had stood until it was sold, dismantled, and carted away to pay Tolstoy's youthful gambling debts. Tolstoy, his slim, dark-eyed wife, Sonya (who was only twenty-one), their three small children (Sergei, Tatyana, and Ilya), his aunt, and his aunt's companion lived in the house on the right, and it was modest enough: five rooms downstairs, five upstairs, whitewashed walls inside, unvarnished floors, most chairs unupholstered. No matter. Tolstoy was not interested in tidiness or display. He was rethinking the concept of his unfinished novel, a second part of which had just been published in the February, March, and April issues of *The Russian Herald* and the title of which he would change in November from *The Year 1805* to *War and Peace*. He had other problems. He complained of high blood pressure, stomach pains, and "noises in the head." There were days when the children got on his nerves, and at times he shouted angrily at his wife. Sonya, having been brought up in the Kremlin in Moscow (her father was a doctor), found it irritatingly difficult to live with the burdocks that grew all about, the trash the peasant cook threw from the kitchen window, and the persistent smell of manure from the barns and barnyard. Nevertheless, possibly because familiar faces promised some relief from the

22

tensions of the moment, he welcomed the horsemen when they rode up to the house. They were army officers, as he had been in the Crimean war. As he had done, they wore the uniform of the tsar: peaked caps, white linen jackets, green pants stuffed into polished black boots, white suede gloves.

Could they speak to Tolstoy in private? He had no objection. They were an odd couple but he knew them well. Ever since the Sixty-fifth Moscow Infantry Regiment had come into the area to guard about five hundred convicts who were building a section of the Moscow–Kiev rail line, they had frequently gone riding or hunting with Tolstoy: the older man, Alexander Stasyulevich, because he had known Tolstoy as a soldier in the Caucasus thirteen years before; the younger man, Grigori (Grisha) Kolokoltsov, because he had gone to cadet school with Sonya's older brother. Stasyulevich was a sour-faced fellow, about thirty-six, and an ensign, the lowest commissioned rank in the army. Kolokoltsov was an easygoing, genial lad, about twenty-one, and a second lieutenant, pleased with himself and his life in the service. Stasyulevich did the talking.

Did Tolstoy remember their telling him about a private in their Second Company who faced court-martial and death by firing squad for striking his captain? Tolstoy remembered. He remembered anything that had to do with the death penalty. And did he recall they felt there were extenuating circumstances that the regulations should but did not recognize? Tolstoy remembered.

Well, something had come up. Their regimental commander, Colonel Yunosha, who also often went riding and hunting with Tolstoy, had just named them, along with himself, officers of the court. Despite their feelings in the matter, they would have to sit in judgment, with little freedom of action.

What could Tolstoy do about it?

23

He could serve as counsel for the defense, fight for the soldier's life, argue the case in such a way that they could vote not guilty or for some punishment short of death. Would he serve?

It was a startling question, though understandable. Tolstoy was a civilian, but he knew the army, having served in the Caucasus as Stasyulevich had done, on the Danube against the Turks, and as a lieutenant of artillery in the dangerous Fourth Bastion at Sevastopol. He knew something about the law, having studied it for two years at Kazan University and passed two legal examinations in St. Petersburg. Furthermore, he was an aristocrat, a count, a landowner, and a successful writer, and his vigorous opposition to capital punishment was widely known. Other penalties for violation of the law Tolstoy understood. Solitary confinement in the Fortress of Peter and Paul in St. Petersburg, where men and women often went mad or died of consumption, he accepted without protest; there was nothing he could do about that. Exile to Siberia, where men and women worked for years in leg irons or chained to wheelbarrows, he tolerated; it was an old Russian custom. But the death sentence, except for murder in the course of revolutionary terrorism or an attempt on the life of the tsar, was beyond his comprehension. One who has never seen an execution may feel or believe that capital punishment is morally defensible or that it serves some necessary or useful purpose. Tolstoy did not, for he had watched the deed done during a trip to France nine years before. On March 26, 1857, he had witnessed in Paris the guillotining of one François Richeux for robbery and murder, and his reaction to that bloody sight was swift, instinctive, strong, and lasting.

"I rose before seven and went to see an execution," he wrote in his diary the next day. "A stout, healthy neck and breast. The man kissed the Gospels, and then—death. How senseless! It made a deep impression which will not be wasted. I am not a man of politics. Morals and art I know and love—they are within my powers. The guillotine kept me long from sleeping and made me reflect."[2]

On the same day, with the vision of the slashing, flashing blade still sharp in his mind, he wrote to his friend Vasili Botkin, the Russian literary critic:

> I witnessed many atrocities in the war and in the Caucasus, but I should have been less sickened to see a man torn to pieces before my eyes than I was by this perfected, elegant machine, by means of which a strong, clean, healthy man was killed in an instant. In the first case there is no reasoning will, but a paroxysm of human passion; in the second, coolness to the point of refinement, homicide-with-comfort, nothing big. A cynical, insolent determination to do justice, obey the law of God—justice as proclaimed by lawyers, who make utterly contradictory allegations in the name of honor, religion and truth. . . . Human law—what a farce! . . . I shall never enter the service of any government anywhere.[3]

He was then twenty-eight years old.

Would Tolstoy take the case?

There were difficulties. He had not finished his legal studies. He had never worked in a law office or in a legal department of the government. He had never appeared before a military court, and although he usually wrote little in summer, he had his novel to think about, and it was going to take longer than he had believed a few months before. Where would the trial be held?

In Yasenki, a few miles to the south.

When?

On July 16.

How long would it last?

A few hours at most.

In the published record there is no indication that Tolstoy

hesitated more than briefly, if at all. Yes, he'd appear before the court. He'd need Colonel Yunosha's permission and, of course, copies of the indictment and the military regulations. But having heard the mitigating circumstances (among other things, the accused was said to have been drunk when he committed the crime) and having questioned Stasyulevich and Kolokoltsov, Tolstoy had reasons to think he might get him off. The reasons apparently were these: first, the offended captain was a Pole, and Russians didn't like Poles any more than Poles liked Russians; second, Colonel Yunosha, his frequent guest and companion, would preside at the trial; third, Stasyulevich and Kolokoltsov would be the only other officers of the court; and fourth—an intriguingly persuasive point—all he needed to win were the votes of two of the three judges.

With these wild cards in his hand, Tolstoy set out for regimental headquarters the next day.

2

The Crime and the Punishment

Private Vasili Shabunin, of the Second Company, First Battalion, Sixty-fifth Moscow Infantry Regiment, was twenty-four years old, of less than average height, stocky to fat, with rust-colored hair and a thick, red neck. His face, according to a witness to the scene that is about to be described, "did not give an especially pleasing appearance" (Biryukov), and he is said to have been "of very limited intelligence" (Maude) and an "imbecile" (Troyat).[1] Tolstoy said as much at the trial, but he spoke to influence the officers of the court and not necessarily out of conviction.

Granted that Shabunin was an eccentric, a loner, and an alcoholic. His idea of bliss was to lie on his bunk when the day's work was done, sip *sivukha*—a raw local brandy—or vodka, and recite the Psalms and Gospels, which he is said to have known by heart. But a fool? He could read and write, an accomplishment so rare in those days that many merchants and tradesmen in St. Petersburg, Moscow, and all Russia announced their wares with wordless outdoor signs: the picture of a fish for a fish market, of a hammer and nails for a carpenter's shop, and so on. He was also an unusual soldier who showed some aptitude for army life. For one thing, he was an *okhotnik*, a volunteer; that is, at a time when the length of compulsory military service was a back-breaking twenty-five years (for all but Jews, who were explicitly excluded by the regulations, the term could be reduced to fifteen years for exceptional service), he took the place of a draftee. (The going rate paid to a replacement by a drafted man or members of his family was 300 rubles or $150, though some men volunteered for nothing to save a brother or friend with small children.) For another, Shabunin rose to the rank of sergeant in the Ekaterinoslav (Dnepropetrovsk) Life Grenadiers before his transfer to the Sixty-fifth. His promotions also suggest that he was not so dull-witted as he is said to have been.

He was, however, in deep trouble. Something about Captain Yasevich, his Polish commander, irritated Shabunin, and something about Shabunin irritated Captain Yasevich, with the result that not long after the regiment arrived in the vicinity of Yasnaya Polyana he was stripped of his rank and jailed briefly for a minor infraction of the regulations. Thereafter, Shabunin took to drink with increasing enthusiasm, and it was evidently with drink in mind that he left camp on his morning off. That was a Monday, the sixth of June. Shabunin walked to Yasenki, near Tolstoy's estate, or to Ozerki, another dusty village four miles farther to the south, and there bought from the local liquor store a *shtof* of vodka. A *shtof* was a measure equal to about one and a third quarts.

One wonders what he thought about in the early hours of that critical day. About the loss of his sergeant's stripes and the pay that went with them? About his Polish captain, who was giving him a hard time? About the ominous years in the army that stretched before him, nearly a lifetime?

Perhaps he reflected on childhood dreams of adventure, fame, and fortune, for although he was officially a *meshchanin*, one of the lower middle class, his family was relatively well-to-do, and with its assistance he might have hoped to budge the doors of opportunity. Perhaps, too,

The Crime and the Punishment

there came to mind an official report he had copied a few days before about the execution of a soldier for striking a superior. No one knows. He was never asked.

Shabunin sipped the vodka; how much he drank is uncertain, but not all of it, because when he went on duty at noon he hid what was left in the anteroom of the *izba* or peasant's hut that served as headquarters of the Second Company. He then walked in to face his hated captain, a graduate of the General Staff Academy, who was said to have been a disciplinarian though cool of manner and soft of voice. Captain Yasevich gave him a report to copy out for the battalion commander and left the hut.

Shabunin was now alone with the problems that were beginning to overwhelm him. For weeks the captain had been riding him. For weeks the captain, demanding perfection, had made him do his work over and over again. So it is quite likely, as was later alleged, that he paused in his writing from time to time that afternoon and stepped out for a drink or two. But he completed the report, and it was in Shabunin's opinion in excellent shape when Yasevich returned about five o'clock, accompanied as usual by the sergeant major.

This was the decisive moment. Yasevich glanced casually at the report, then sat down to read it with care. As he did so, Shabunin went to the anteroom, where the vodka was concealed. When he returned, his face flushed, so it is said, the captain rose, crumpled the report in his hand, and threw it in Shabunin's face.

Something snapped inside the young redhead. He uttered an insulting remark, which is not recorded. That was enough for the captain, who turned to the sergeant major and said in that quiet voice of his: "He is drunk again. Lock him up, and when the day's work is done, get the birch rods ready."[2] The birch rods meant a hundred strokes over the

29

bare back. With that the captain, slowly pulling on his white suede gloves, walked leisurely out of the hut. Shabunin, his face contorted with resentment and anger, rushed after him.

"Why?" he screamed when he got outside. "Why do you torment me?"

Not deigning to reply, Yasevich, still pulling on his gloves, looked icily at the maddened soldier.

Shabunin in the manner of all outraged and desperate men lost control of himself. "Silence!" he shouted. "You'll beat me with birch rods?" He clenched his fist and swung. "Take that in your Polish mug [*kharya* in Biryukov's account, *morda* in *Pravo's*]." As the captain staggered back, blood flowed from his nose.[3]

That evening Shabunin was locked in a guarded hut at Ozerki, and two documents were prepared, one describing the incident, the other the captain's physical condition. Colonel Yunosha moved swiftly. That same night he ordered an immediate investigation and the next day sent the results to Adjutant General Gildenshtubbe of the Moscow Military District, which had jurisdiction over the Tula region. Several weeks later, at the end of June or in early July, word came back that Shabunin was to be tried by court-martial under Article 604 of the code of military regulations.[4] Article 604 was short and unequivocal: "Raising a hand or weapon against a superior is to be punished by death."

Not "may be" but "is to be." In short, to convict Shabunin, to send him before a firing squad, to snuff out his life, it was not necessary to find that he had struck the captain or intended to strike him, or that he was in full possession of his senses at the moment. The mere "raising a hand," if proved, compelled the imposition of the death penalty.

Soon after they heard they would have to serve as officers of the court, Stasyulevich and Kolokoltsov sought Tolstoy's help.

3

First Talk with the Accused

Tolstoy had no time to spare and spared none. Setting out the next day for regimental headquarters at Yasenki, he first passed through his native village, which was so much a part of his life that he and the loose, gray, homemade blouse he affected blended into the landscape almost as unobtrusively, as casually, as the narrow creek that crossed and often flooded its lone dirt street. This was Tolstoy country. His grandfather and his grandmother on his mother's side and his father and mother had lived here. He had been born here, on August 28, 1828. So had his three older brothers—Nikolai in 1823, Sergei in 1826, and Dmitri in 1827—and his younger sister, Marya, in 1830. In the division of the family property at their father's death, the lucrative farms in the black-earth region to the south had gone to his brothers, Nikolskoye to Nikolai, Pirogovo to Sergei, and Sherbatchevka to Dmitri (by agreement among the four brothers, Marya got a share of Pirogovo). Yasnaya Polyana had come to Leo. So had its peasant and household serfs, and although they were no longer bound to him or anyone else, they still doffed their caps or clutched their forelocks when he rode by. Tolstoy's jurist friend Anatoli Koni understood it was their view that "he has brains even if he is a nobleman."[1]

Yasenki was only three miles to the south, but in the time

it takes to ride that distance a hundred thoughts or impressions can flash through the mind. In a split second one recalls an unforgettable experience, in seconds an entire episode. The sight of a peasant in the fields may have reminded Tolstoy that Alexander II, emperor and tsar, had liberated the serfs five years before (it was "much better," Alexander said, for the abolition of serfdom "to come from above than below"). That had been all right with Tolstoy. He had opposed serfdom in principle, and if many of the men who once worked his fields were now employed for wages in Tula, ten miles to the north, he would get by just the same. He was receiving the profits of the Nikolskoye estate of his late brother Nikolai, who had died in 1860, and money was beginning to come in from the magazine serial rights to his unfinished novel. But the novel wasn't good enough. He would have to raise his sights—as high as Feodor Dostoyevsky had in *Crime and Punishment*, which was appearing at the same time in the same magazine, *The Russian Herald*: Dostoyevsky's in the January, February, April, and June issues, Tolstoy's in the issues of February, March, and April.

The thought changes. The images change. A court-martial. The possibility of death by firing squad. The Paris guillotine. One may speculate that in the eye of the mind he saw the stumbling criminal being led out accompanied by priests, the warden, and prison guards. Perhaps in the ear of the mind he again heard the shouts and exclamations of the excited mob as children were lifted high and necks strained to take in every detail of the bloody act.

Again the thought changes. Again the images change. Did Tolstoy recall that when he was a soldier in the Caucasus, fighting the wild mountain tribesmen of Shamil, the Lion of Daghestan, he had talked with a grim-faced man named Alexander Stasyulevich, the same Stasyulevich who with young Kolokoltsov had just enlisted his help in the Shabunin affair? Did he remember what he wrote in his diary the next day or the first story he published after the Crimean war? The questions arise because in later years he seemed to blur intentionally this early association, as if it were one he wished to forget.

In a diary entry on November 4, 1853, he recorded a conversation at Starogladkovskaya, on the left bank of the Terek, in which Stasyulevich explained how it had come about that the year before, when he was a second lieutenant in His Majesty's Thirteenth Erivan Life Grenadier Regiment, he had been court-martialed and demoted to the ranks.[2] Stasyulevich, Tolstoy noted, had been officer of the guard at Metekhov prison in Tbilisi (Tiflis), Georgia, when, unknown to him, another officer and a noncommissioned officer were bribed to let out six Muslim prisoners to commit robbery on behalf of a Georgian prince who was friendly to the Russians. An improbable story, you may believe, but one with painful consequences, which Tolstoy drew upon for a tale he first called *A Degraded Officer* and then, when the censors got through with it, *Meeting a Moscow Acquaintance in the Detachment*. The point of Tolstoy's story was that an officer such as Stasyulevich, one of the untitled nobility, who is stripped of his commission and forced to serve as a common soldier, suffers horribly; jeered at by his former comrades and rejected by the men in the ranks, he deteriorates. Stasyulevich had suffered horribly, and although he again held a commission, having been pardoned by the tsar, he was in the humiliating position of being the most junior officer in the regiment of Colonel Yunosha, his classmate and friend from cadet days. Colonel Yunosha was a hardheaded professional soldier, the kind who never makes a minor mistake; a thick-set, ruddy-faced bachelor who felt he had an irresistible case against Private Shabunin.

Tolstoy arrives at Yasenki. Yunosha receives him affably. He readily agrees to Tolstoy's serving as counsel for the defense and gives him a copy of the indictment, which Shabunin has not yet seen. He consents to Tolstoy's meeting with Shabunin before the trial and sends Stasyulevich or Kolokoltsov to accompany him.

Tolstoy rides on to Ozerki, but he has a clearer understanding now of the burden he is assuming. Comforting as it is to know that Stasyulevich and Kolokoltsov constitute a majority of the court, it is awesomely clear from the indictment that Shabunin has confessed. It is also clear that he signed a confession dictated to him by an investigator for Colonel Yunosha.

Years later, when he came to describe his first meeting with Shabunin, Tolstoy was uncharacteristically brief for a writer with acute powers of observation and an exceptional knowledge of human nature. In the letter he wrote to Biryukov in 1908, one senses with suspicion a touch of intentional restraint, which brings to mind Dryden's remark in *The Hind and the Panther*: "Secret guilt by silence is betrayed."

I recall [Tolstoy told Biryukov] that having arrived at Ozerki village, where the accused was held (I do not remember whether the crime was committed there or in another place), and having entered a low, brick *izba*, I was met by a young man with prominent cheekbones, more stout than lean, which is very rare for a soldier, with a simple, expressionless face. I do not recall whom I was with—Kolokoltsov, it seems. When we entered, he stood at attention. I told him I wanted to be his counsel and asked him to tell me what happened. He spoke little of his own accord and only in reply to my questions answered reluctantly: "Precisely" [*tak tochno*]. The sense of his answers was that he was bored and that his company commander was demanding. "He leaned on me," he said.[3]

From this terse account it appears that Tolstoy took the redhead for a total idiot, without considering the possibility that in signing a confession the day after the crime and refusing to participate in his own defense, Shabunin was electing to let military justice run its course. One cannot be certain, however. When Tolstoy wrote to Biryukov, he was concerned not with Shabunin's thinking—it had happened so long ago—but with his own role in the affair; not with whether Shabunin sought death by firing squad but with man's inhumanity to man, the ways of the law, and the distinction between justice and the law. Moreover, in his plea to the military court he circled all around a suggestion of suicide, as if he wanted to speak of it but dared not for fear of destroying his case.

There is, however, support for the suicide theory. Charles T. H. Wright, secretary and librarian of the London Library, who was related to one of Tolstoy's daughters-in-law and wrote the article about him in the eleventh edition of the *Encyclopaedia Britannica* (1911), said without qualification that Shabunin sought death to escape a worse fate, and the customs of the time lend force to his statement. Against it, to be sure, is the very concept of suicide, which, however comprehensible to the few who have had any association with it, is foreign to the many who cannot apprehend an act that puts an end to the only life one knows. Since the dawn of history human beings have preferred hardship and the most intolerable conditions of servitude to death, and yet suicide occurs and takes strange forms. I knew an American sergeant in World War II who put a stop to excruciating headaches by climbing out of a foxhole and standing upright in a field of German machine-gun fire. To understand Shabunin, then, it is useful to look more closely at the army he served in and the punishments other than death he could have expected.

The army in those days—and conditions were no better or little more so in some other European forces—was more like a penal colony than anything else, a private treated not much better than a convict. A man "sent for a soldier," as

Some Call It Murder

the expression went, was looked upon by family, friends, and neighbors as a man sentenced to death. Professional wailers expressed the grief of wife and children. Special laments, called *prichitaniya*, were sung as the illiterate recruit left home with head and beard shaved (in an early version of *Polikushka*, Tolstoy quoted the words of one of them: "My handsome falcon, / Your dear hair will be cut. / They are going to shave you. / They are going to destroy / your beauty . . .").[4] He would be gone for twenty-five years, barring a near miracle, and his wife would become a *soldatka*, virtually a widow. Privileged men had access to cadet schools and commissions, while the ranks were filled with conscripts drawn from the peasantry and the urban poor. Another source of coerced manpower was the judicial system and the sentences it imposed on "politicals" and common criminals: novelists and murderers, poets and burglars, editors and arsonists, publishers and pickpockets. The novelists Dostoyevsky and Alexander Bestuzhev (Marlinsky) and the poets Mikhail Lermontov, Alexander Odoyevsky, Taras Shevchenko and Alexander Polezhayev were "sent for soldiers," Dostoyevsky for three years to the Seventh Siberian Battalion as Semipalatinsk after he had been confined for eight months in the Fortress of Peter and Paul and four years at hard labor in the prison at Omsk. Polezhayev was ordered to a regiment of the line for his poem *Sashka*, which protested the evils of autocracy, and he was not pardoned by the tsar until years later, when he lay dying in a Moscow hospital. As a further act of imperial grace, Polezhayev was commissioned an officer posthumously.

Once in the army, men were exposed to brutality and barbarous humiliation. Officers punched them, knocked them down, kicked them, called them fools, dogs, idiots, and pigs. An officer who shrank from such disciplinary methods was considered too softhearted for command and eased out of the service. A soldier had no recourse. If he protested, he got the knout, the rods, or the club, means of corporal punishment that, according to law, could not be inflicted upon civilians (not by 1866). Company officers had to be addressed as "Your Honor," field officers as "Your High Honor," counts (such as Tolstoy) and princes as "Your Illustriousness," generals and marshals as "Your High Excellency." Stasyulevich knew; he had been through it.

Military justice, as it was called, was uneven and arbitrary. To discourage desertion when the runaway rate was high, a man could get death or confinement, chained to a wall, in a steaming prison or freezing fortress. When the rate was relatively low, the rods were applied, and that punishment could be inflicted time and again for the same offense. For being absent without leave to present a petition for pardon to the tsar, Polezhayev was convicted of desertion and sentenced to a thousand strokes, a hundred at a time.

The gauntlet, which was much more severe than the gauntlet of early American history, was abolished a few weeks or months before Shabunin struck Yasevich, so recently that at the time of the Shabunin affair General Dmitri Milyutin, the minister of war, had to be reminded that it was no longer an available punishment. In Russia—as in Prussia, where the punishment is said to have originated— no man "ran the gauntlet"; he was "driven through the ranks" (*prognaniem skvoz stroi*) of 500 men, 250 on a side, each with a club or stick in his hand. (Tolstoy describes the punishment, which was known as "walking the green street," in *Nicholas Stick* and *After the Ball*, which was based on a true incident known to Leo and his brother Sergei when they were students at Kazan University.) The victim's hands and wrists were tied to the rifle barrels of two noncommissioned officers, who, while the regimental band played a mournful tune, walked slowly backward before him, pulling him along, their bayonets touching his breast so that he would be impaled if he quickened his step. Behind him walked an officer who was quick to order other noncoms, standing behind the ranks, to club any man who failed to strike forcefully enough.

In theory (according to the regulations), there was a limit to the number of times a man could be driven through the ranks for the same offense: once for looting the pockets of the dead during an engagement (Article 637), twice for looting the pockets of the (Russian) wounded (Article 638), and so on. In practice, however, a regiment in the field did pretty much as it pleased, and death "by accident" not infrequently resulted.

There were stiffer sentences. There were punishment battalions where life was hell and was intended to me. There was exile at hard labor in the most horrifying convict camps in Siberia. And the likelihood is that if the former had been his fate, Shabunin would not have lived long; if the latter, he would have been marched on foot to distant Siberia, where with leg irons attached and his body branded he would have been chained to a wheelbarrow for the rest of his life.

After seeing Shabunin, the redhead who was so reluctant to assist in his own defense, Tolstoy rode back to Yasnaya Polyana; and that week or the next he set aside his work on *War and Peace* and wrote out his plea to the court, which for all its flaws was an ingenious effort for its time.

4

Tolstoy before the Trial

Word that a soldier was about to be tried for his life spread swiftly through the rolling Russian countryside, with the result that by dawn on the morning of the trial, Wednesday, July 16, there was fussy activity in the homes of distant landowners as far away as Tula, the district capital, ten miles to the north of Yasnaya Polyana and thirteen miles from Yasenki. Usually in that month and at that hour only peasants were up and about, having a glass of tea and a chunk of dark bread, perhaps a little cabbage, a cucumber, or an onion; it was haying time, and the harvest was approaching. Then for a few crushing weeks they would be lucky to sleep more than three or four hours a night. But on this day there was also movement in the houses of the rich and otherwise privileged. A court-martial was an event not to be missed, and Tolstoy's role in the affair promised a memorable performance. Landowners who liked or respected him (and there were not many) were eager to see him in action against the power of the state, with which he had quarreled before, and once in a while had won. Others, who viewed him as a traitor to his class, hoped to see him get what they felt had long been coming to him. As *mirovoi posrednik* or arbiter of the peace soon after the emancipation of the serfs, he had been vexingly fair in ruling on the many disputes that arose between them and their liberated peasants. Accordingly, preparations for a ride to Yasenki were soon under way. Candles, brightly burning, obscured the cupped flames that flickered before the icons. Servants lighted fires in the samovars. Grooms watered and fed the horses. Carriages were greased.

There is, however, no indication of excitement that morning at Yasnaya Polyana. The court-martial was fixed for eleven o'clock, and although Tolstoy planned another talk with Shabunin before the proceedings opened—to calm him, he said later, and perhaps to explain to the accused and win his support for the arguments on which he would base his defense—there was no need to hurry. In any case, something was always going on at sunrise on the Tolstoy estate. It was a big place. He had woods, fields, ponds, a dairy farm, sheep, pigs, horses, an apiary with a blind beekeeper, a coachman, an antique cook (once a flute player in his grandfather's orchestra of serfs, who had been banished to the kitchen because he lost his mouthpiece), an assistant cook, a valet and steward (Alexei Orekhov, one of the two serfs he took with him as batmen when he went to the wars), a nurse, a chambermaid, a laundress, someone to watch out for the dogs, a cowherd, and a bailiff (to prevent the peasants from cutting down his trees for firewood). On such a farm there is always someone at work at an early hour, and Tolstoy, one imagines, would have seen no need to rouse the household just because he was going to Yasenki to address a military court. He was good and knew he was good at about anything that fascinated him, and if, on awakening, he read over his plea to the court, he might have made a few corrections—no more. It was not intended to be a literary effort. All he sought was an appropriate mixture of fact, legal sophistry, and emotional appeal, and he had that. He would see Shabunin at ten o'clock.

But let us look a little more intently at this extraordinary

Russian, who, because he was horrified and disgusted by the death penalty, was assuming a burden that over the years would affect him more than anyone he knew would realize or acknowledge. Leo Tolstoy—Leo Tolstoy of the compelling eyes—was a restless, sensitive, contradictory man with a studied glare and a perceptive ear, inquisitive, hard-working, meticulous in some ways, overly casual in others, independent-minded, opinionated, ill-tempered when it suited him, unusually engaging when he wanted to be. Turgenev called him a troglodyte because of "his barbaric ardor and bullheadedness."[1]

He had decided likes and dislikes. He was in love with his tall, dark, and handsome wife, Sonya, who at twenty-one was sixteen years his junior, but he resisted her efforts to change him, to turn him into something he was not, to refine his manners and country dress, and she had an annoying habit of complaining about the way of life he knew best. He enjoyed his son Sergei, who was three years old, his daughter Tatyana, who soon would be two, and, though not keenly, his son Ilya, who was not yet two months. He had decided ideas about children. In his view, they should learn to depend on themselves, and for this reason he objected to their playing with store-bought toys.

He was powerfully attracted to the gypsy and peasant girls who caught his eye but hated himself in the morning, and in some ways he was astonishingly proper. "When traveling," he once said, "a respectable woman must be dressed in a *costume tailleur* in black or some other dark color—with a matching bag, wear gloves, and carry a French or English novel."[2]

His interests were amazingly wide: farming, education, and writing, of course, but also riding, hunting, skating, playing cards, breeding pigs, singing, playing the piano, entertaining house guests, playing pool, studying philosophy, learning foreign languages (he spoke French, English, and German), keeping abreast of scientific knowledge and achievements, hearing and capturing the colorful expressions of common people, planting trees, cultivating flowers, observing the impact of the changing seasons on his surroundings, and reading. He kept his books and manuscripts under lock and key.

There was also much that evidently did not interest him: foreign affairs, national affairs, what was going on in Moscow and St. Petersburg, how the writer Nikolai Chernyshevsky, who was serving a sentence at hard labor in Siberia, or the literary critic Dmitri Pisarev, who was confined in the Fortress of Peter and Paul, were getting along. He cared little for the opinions of Ivan Turgenev, whom he had challenged to a duel in 1861 and who had challenged him in return. Although nothing had come of that angry dispute, the two men had not seen each other or exchanged letters since. In the summer of 1866 Turgenev was living in Baden Baden, writing *Smoke*. Tolstoy had no wish to—and never did—meet or exchange letters with Dostoyevsky, the troubled epileptic who had returned from Siberian exile almost nine years before. Dostoyevsky was in a terrible fix that summer. Deep in debt from gambling, on June 1 he signed a contract with the Moscow publisher Feodor Stellovsky, selling for little money the rights to all his prior works and promising delivery of a new novel by November 1. If he failed to deliver, Stellovsky would acquire the rights to all his future works. (Dostoyevsky met the deadline. On October 5 he began to dictate *The Gambler* to Anna Snitkin, whom he later married, and he turned in the finished manuscript on time.)

And yet for all his quirks and eccentricities, his likes and dislikes, his interests and shortcomings, Tolstoy at thirty-seven was a creative genius, a natural-born writer with a remarkable talent for portraying his fictional characters by revealing their innermost feelings. Tolstoy the man said what he pleased, whether his listeners liked it or not, but Tolstoy the writer refrained from rhetorical virtuosity. To achieve the effect he sought, he wrote, crossed out, rewrote, and repeated the process again and again. Like every good editor, he knew that one improved a story more by cutting it back than by adding to it. He also knew there was no short cut to excellence. "Inspiration," he used to say, "comes from writing."

On writing days he labored in his room, scratching out in a small, almost illegible hand the lines that Sonya would have to decipher when she came to copy them for the printers. Other days he passed on the farm, in the saddle, or in long walks through the neighborhood, with a notebook handy so he could jot down observations for future use: the whirring sound of a woodcock's wings, the habits of a nightingale, the color of a puddle in the road on a clear or cloudy day, the rhythm of rainwater dripping from an aspen leaf. Going out helped him to think. Going out made it easier to support the headaches that afflicted him and the domestic quarrels for which he was in part responsible. As he rode or walked, Tolstoy, more than most men, talked to himself, argued with himself, berated himself for believing one thing and doing another.

On July 16, however, he knew he was acting according to the principles he espoused. If some members of his class disapproved, so much the worse for them. He would face the court with all the power of his intellect and whatever tenacity the circumstances required.

5

Tolstoy's Plea to the Court

It was, I think, with feelings of confidence and mounting excitement that Tolstoy rode out of his estate about nine o'clock that Wednesday morning and turned south—to his right—through his native village on the Yasenki road. The confidence I infer from the fact that before the day was out and in an unusual gesture he would give a reporter from the Tula weekly newspaper a copy of his plea to the court, which he had in his pocket or a saddlebag.[1] The sense of excitement I gather from the fact this was his first appearance in court and that he had spoken only once before in public—seven years before, when he addressed the Society of Lovers of Russian Literature in Moscow.

I see him, then, easy in the saddle, preoccupied with his own thoughts, and almost oblivious of others on the move that day. If he noticed them at all, he would have glanced hastily and with contempt at the well-dressed men of Tula who were going to the trial by carriage or on horseback. If they caught his attention, he would have observed with the lack of interest one shows to unprepossessing hitchhikers those wanderers who, before the coming of the railroad, walked the highways and byways of Russia at all hours of the day, most of them with *lapti* or bark shoes on their feet and rough-cut walking staffs in their hands. They were the troubled, the uprooted, the eccentric, the impoverished, and men and women careful with their rubles and kopecks: the sick, the well, the hopeless, and the hopeful, workers sentenced to or returning from exile, peasants heading for what they had heard (wrongly) were the greener pastures of Asia, holy men, pilgrims, religious dissenters of one kind or another, tramps, peddlers, professional storytellers, circus performers, students, soldiers on leave. Tolstoy had seen them ever since he could remember.

At Yasenki he pulled up at regimental headquarters, which were lodged in a mansion owned by an absentee landlord. Already an expectant crowd, which included his neighbor Alexander Bibikov, was gathering. Tolstoy must have been pleased to see Bibikov, a widower and small landowner who lived with his housekeeper, Anna Pirogov, and his two sons at Telyatinki, a mile or so from Yasnaya Polyana. The two men often went hunting together and were joint owners of a vodka distillery. (When in 1872 Bibikov dropped his housekeeper and made the boys' governess his mistress, Anna ran away and threw herself under a train at Yasenki station, leaving a letter for Bibikov in which she wrote: "You are my murderer. Be happy if an assassin can be happy. If you like, you can see my corpse on the rails at Yasenki."[2] Hearing of her death, Tolstoy hurried to the station, took notes, and later drew on the scene for the suicide of Anna Karenina.)

Tolstoy now had work to do. He saw Colonel Yunosha, met a special prosecutor who had come down from Moscow (a bad sign), and had a talk with Shabunin, who was locked in a temporary guardhouse. Shabunin, it would seem, saw himself as a plaything in the hands of powerful, selfish, vindictive men, with no possibility of being saved even with the help of this count who was unknown to him. Tolstoy saw things differently. He had, after all, been asked to take the case by two members of the court.

Military justice grinds inexorably and with a punctuality

that is regarded as one of the redeeming features of the system. Shortly before eleven o'clock the three judges filed into the drawing room and took their seats on three sides of a rectangular table: Colonel Yunosha, ruddy-faced as always, in the center, facing the spectators; Lieutenant Kolokoltsov, looking very young, to his right; Ensign Stasyulevich, melancholy as usual, to his left. The talking stopped. A hush fell over the room. As the prisoner was brought in, flanked by two armed guards, men straightened in their chairs and stared at the judges, none of them more searchingly, I imagine, than Tolstoy, for Yunosha, it seems, was one of the few men who puzzled him. Tolstoy's children say in their memoirs that he was a difficult person to fool, impossible to lie to successfully (something like Alpatych in *War and Peace*, who says to Dron: "I can see through you and three yards [*arshins*] into the ground under you)."[3] But of Yunosha he wrote years later to Biryukov: "Judging from the human point of view, it is impossible to say of such a man whether he is good, whether he is reasonable, because one does not know what he would be like if he stopped being a colonel, a professor, a [cabinet] minister, a judge, or a journalist and stood forth as a man. So it was with Colonel Yunosha. He was an industrious regimental commander, a proper guest, but what kind of man he was it was impossible to say. I think he himself did not know and was not interested [in finding out]."[4]

Yunosha called the court to order. No need to waste time. The special prosecutor rose and read the indictment. The crime, he said, was premeditated and carried out by an angered man who drank vodka to stimulate his courage. To demolish the defense before it had an opportunity to speak, he called the regimental physician. The regimental physician declared he had examined Shabunin and found him legally sane.

Whether Shabunin was asked to do much more than acknowledge his confession is uncertain. The prosecution appears to have asked a few questions to bring out its salient points. Had he so confessed? Had he confessed accurately? Did he wish to change his testimony? and so on. But the record, in so far as it has been published, makes no mention of his examination by the judges or, for that matter, by Tolstoy for the defense. It does say that as the prosecutor demanded the death penalty, Shabunin, standing up between the guards, listened impassively, apathetically, as if the proceedings concerned someone other than himself.

It was Tolstoy's turn, and although the evidence and the law were against him, he fought stubbornly for the life of the young man he had seen only once before this day. Later on, at a more mature age, he would have challenged the entire system, based his case not on military law but on the moral law and the law of God (so he wrote to Biryukov in 1908), but he was young then and still willing, however reluctantly, to acknowledge that society or the state or the army had the right as well as the power to kill one of its own.

Tolstoy stood up, all five feet eight of him, and the plea in his hand, though flawed by repetition and clearly less effective than it might have been if he had had more time to prepare it, reflected both conviction and originality of thought. So far as I know, it has not been published before in English.

Tolstoy said: "Private Vasili Shabunin, who is charged with knowingly and intentionally striking his company commander in the face, chose me to defend him, and I accepted the responsibility although the crime of which he is accused is one of those that, breaking the bond of military discipline, must always be punished, and cannot be viewed from the standpoint of whether the punishment is commensurate with the crime. I accepted this responsibility despite the fact that the accused wrote out his own confession, which establishes the fact of his guilt beyond any possibility of refutation, and also despite the fact that he is being tried under Article Six-o-four of the military code, which decrees only one punishment for the crime committed by Shabunin.

"That punishment is death, and this is why it would appear his fate cannot be alleviated. But I took on his defense because our law, which is written in the spirit that it is better to forgive ten guilty men than punish one who is innocent, makes every provision for mercy and determines not for the sake of mere formality that no accused person may be brought to trial without someone to defend him; that is to say, without the possibility of acquittal or a lessening of the punishment. It is, then, with assurance that I proceed to his formal defense. In my judgment the accused is subject to Articles One-o-nine and One-sixteen, which provide for reduced punishment on a showing of dullness or stupidity on the part of the criminal [Article 109] and irresponsibility [acquittal] on a showing of insanity [Article 116]."

Here Tolstoy was on unsteady ground, and he evidently knew it, because he did not quote or summarize the articles referred to or seek to demonstrate their applicability. Article 109 specifically excluded a stupidity plea if the accused acted in anger, as the prosecution charged and Shabunin admitted, and Article 116 stated unequivocally that insanity had to be established "according to law," that is, diagnosed by a physician. Unlike the prosecution, Tolstoy had not sought a physician to examine his client. He continued:

"Shabunin does not suffer from continual madness. This is obvious from the doctor's examination. But the state of his mind is abnormal. He is mentally ill. He suffers from the absence of one of the principal faculties of man, the faculty of grasping the consequences of his crime. If the science of mental illness does not recognize this mental state as an illness, I suggest that before a death sentence is pronounced we must look closely at the phenomenon and decide whether what I say is a lame excuse or a valid, obvious fact. On the one hand, the condition of the accused is one of extreme stupidity, simplemindedness, and dullness that warrants a reduction of punishment because it is covered by Article One-o-nine. On the other hand, at a given moment, influenced by alcohol, excited to action, his condition is one of insanity covered by Article One-sixteen."

Tolstoy turned his sharp eyes toward the prisoner's dock. Shabunin was still on his feet.

"There he stands before you with downcast eyes. His countenance is indifferent, composed, and dull. He expects the death penalty, yet not a muscle of his face trembles during the questioning or my defense, nor will one tremble during the announcement of a death sentence or even at the moment such a sentence is carried out. His face is immobile not by an effort of will on his part but because of the total absence of spiritual life in this unfortunate man. He is mentally [morally?] asleep as he has been all his life. He does not understand the significance of the crime he committed or the consequence of it, which he anticipates."

Tolstoy then looked at Shabunin's background and the circumstances of the crime and its aftermath.

"Shabunin," he said, "is a *meshchanin* [one of the lower middle class], the son of [relatively] rich parents for his [social] status. At an early age he was apprenticed to a German and later sent to drawing school. Whether he learned anything we do not know, but we may assume he learned little because what he learned did not enable him to escape military service. [At this time Tolstoy evidently did not know that Shabunin was a volunteer who had taken the place of a drafted man, as the information available to Biryukov later on indicated.][5] In 1855 [here Tolstoy made a mistake or there was a typographical error in the Tula paper or *Pravo*, because Shabunin was only twenty-four in 1866] he entered the army and soon, as his military record shows, ran away, not knowing where to or what for, and then came back. A few years later Shabunin was made a noncommissioned officer, solely, we may suppose, because he could write. From then on, he serves only at headquarters. Soon after his promotion to noncommissioned officer, Shabunin, suddenly and for no reason whatsoever, loses all the privileges of his rank owing to an inexplicable act: he steals from a comrade, not money, nothing of value, nothing concealable, but a full-dress uniform and sword, and he trades them for liquor. These acts, which we learn of from Shabunin's record, are not indications of a normal state of mind on the part of the accused. The accused has no tastes or likings; nothing interests him. When he has money enough and time, he drinks, not with his comrades but alone, as the indictment says. After a second year of service he becomes a habitual drinker. He downs two *shtofs* of vodka a day [more than two and a half quarts]. He does not become livelier or merrier than usual. He becomes as you see him now, only more dull-witted, with a greater lack of initiative and determination."

Because Shabunin's service record is not available, it is impossible to say whether it included allegations of doubtful validity or whether Tolstoy felt the need to overstate his case. It would seem, however, that no man can drink that much vodka a day and long survive.

Tolstoy went on: "Two months ago Shabunin was transferred to the Moscow regiment and assigned to the Second Company as a scribe. His sick mental condition worsens with each passing day and reaches its present state. He becomes completely idiotic. He has the appearance of a man but none of the characteristics and interests of a man. For whole days this physically healthy, active person sits in a stuffy *izba* in thirty degrees of heat [86 degrees Fahrenheit] and writes incessantly, again and again, all day long, one or two reports. All Shabunin's interests are concentrated on the words of the reports and on the demands of his superiors. He has no time to eat or sleep. The work does not oppress him. It merely brings on greater stupefaction. But he is satisfied with his position and tells his comrades it is considerably better here than in the Ekaterinoslav Life Grenadiers, from which he was transferred."

Tolstoy was appealing to the regimental pride of the Sixty-fifth. Implying that Shabunin bore no grudge against anyone, he refrained from overt criticism of Captain Yasevich. On the contrary: "Also, he has no reason to complain about his company commander, who says to him more than once (Shabunin told me so himself): 'If you do not have time, get one or two scribes to help you.'

"He passes his days in solitary drunkenness or in the office of his company commander or in the anteroom, where he waits long hours. He writes and drinks, and the state of his mind reaches the point of extreme derangement."

Tolstoy was building his case slowly. "At this time," he went on, "there enters his foggy head a single thought about the narrow sphere of activity within which he revolves. It gathers strength and persistence to the point of madness. He suddenly gets the idea that the company commander understands nothing about the work, the art of writing a report, the pride of every scribe—that he, Shabunin, writes well, writes excellently, whereas the company commander, not knowing the job, compels him to correct and rewrite and, making a mess of his work, adds to it, often leaving him with no time to eat or sleep. This one thought, entering a dull brain that is confused by wine [vodka] and influenced by wounded pride, by the incessantly repeated demands of his company commander, and by continuous contact with him—this thought, born of bitterness, attains in the sick soul of the accused the form of impassioned madness.

"Ask him why—for what reason—he committed the act. He will tell you—and this is the only point about which this man who is being condemned to die speaks with animation and warmth—he will tell you, as he wrote in his affidavit, that the motive for the deed was the frequent demand of his company commander that he rewrite his documents, a job about which the company commander presumably knew less than he, Shabunin, did; or he will say, as he said [in reply] to my question why he committed the crime, he will say: 'Being of sound mind, I decided to do it because *they* do not understand the work, yet *they* are demanding, and that seemed offensive to me.' "

Tolstoy was trying valiantly to lay the foundations for a major point, but it was not easy. The confession was a stubborn obstacle.

"So, gentlemen, the only reason this crime, which is punishable by death, was committed is that it seemed offensive to the accused to rewrite reports on the orders of superiors who knew less about the work than he did. Neither the investigation nor the court nor Shabunin's naive testimony could disclose any other motive. Can one assume that a man in possession of his mental faculties would commit such a terrible crime for this reason—[a crime] terrible in itself as in its consequences—because it seemed to him offensive to rewrite reports? A man who commits such a crime for such a reason is mentally sick, and the defendant is such a man. If the doctor's certificate does not recognize him as such, it is only because medicine does not recognize a state of stupefaction combined with the irritation brought on by wine.

"Is a man who expects death but speaks passionately before the court only of his clerical pride, which has been outraged by his company commander, who, not understanding what has been written, orders him to rewrite—is he really of sound mind?

"Is a man who can read and knows the law, who writes on the sixth or seventh [of June] the confession we have just heard—a confession that deliberately and inescapably gives himself over to death—is he really of sound mind?"

Here, taking advantage of the conventional notion that

there is a connection between insanity and suicide, he seemed to be saying that the confession was a suicidal act.

"It is obvious he penned it in his own hand in words dictated by the investigator, words he confirmed by saying, 'Precisely, Your Honor.' It is obvious that even now, foolishly and unconsciously, he is ready to corroborate anything suggested to him. Why, in the whole Russian empire there is not a man, not a scribe, not even an illiterate muzhik who would give such testimony the day after a crime.

"And what would induce a literate man to give such testimony? If he were not an idiot, he would realize that confession would not lessen the punishment. And repentance could not have provoked the confession because the crime is not one of those that torture the conscience and call for the solace of candid confession. Only a man deprived of the faculty of determining the consequences of his acts, a man psychically ill, would make such a confession. Shabunin's avowal is the surest evidence of the sick state of his mental condition."

That was it. That was his point: anyone who confesses to a crime that is punishable by death is *ipso facto* insane; being insane, he is irresponsible by definition; being irresponsible, he cannot be held accountable for his confession or anything else.

Tolstoy sought to drive his point home: "Finally, is a man who commits a crime under the circumstances Shabunin did—is he really of sound mind? He is a scribe. As a scribe he knew the law, which punishes by death the raising of a hand against a superior, and he knew it all the more because a few days before he committed the crime he wrote out in his own hand an order of the corps directing that a private be shot for raising a hand against a superior. In spite of that, he committed the crime in the presence of the sergeant major, soldiers, and strangers. In the act of the accused one perceives not only a lack of thought and awareness but an act that was clearly carried out in the absence of mental faculties, in a fit of rage, or out of idiocy.

"Constantly rewriting and strongly resenting the ignorance of his company commander, after a sleepless night, drunk on wine, he sits alone before his papers at headquarters and dozes away, relentlessly thinking, as the insane do, about the insulting demands and ignorance of his company commander, when suddenly the company commander walks in—the person most closely associated with his madness and against whom his bitterness, nourished by solitary drinking, is concentrated; and that person again reproaches him and punishes him. Shabunin stands up, still drowsy, not knowing where he is or what he is doing, and commits an act the perpetration of which he cannot account for until later on. [When first questioned, Shabunin said he did not remember what happened. He confessed the next day.]

"Shabunin's past, his appearance, and what he says demonstrate a high degree of obtuseness aggravated by the constant use of wine. His testimony, as if designed to magnify his guilt—indeed the crime itself, which was foolishly committed in the presence of witnesses—shows that there was recently added to his general state of idiocy a state of mental derangement which, if it is not like insanity verifiable by medical examination, it is impossible not to accept as an extenuating circumstance."

All very well, but now Tolstoy had to deal with the law: "Under Article One-o-nine Shabunin is entitled to lesser punishment owing to his obvious idiocy. Moreover, although strictly speaking his case does not come within the scope of Article One-sixteen, Shabunin is entitled to lesser punishment because of the exceptional nature of his mental disorder and because of the article's overall import.

"But Article Six-o-four decrees only one punishment for the crime committed by Shabunin—death. And so in the present case the court is faced with the necessity either of applying literally Article Six-o-four and departing from the spirit of Articles One-o-nine and One-sixteen, which provide for a lesser punishment on a showing that the criminal is in an abnormal state—which Shabunin is—or of applying Articles One-o-nine and One-sixteen, which reduce the punishment, and departing from the spirit of Article Six-o-four. I suggest that the fairer and more valid way out of this difficulty is the latter, because the spirit of Article One-o-nine applies to all articles that follow it, therefore also to Article Six-o-four, nothing being said about its being an exception.

"In the present case the court faces a contradiction between Article One-o-nine, lessening the punishment, and Article Six-o-four, which calls for only one punishment. And it has only two choices. It can back away from the letter of Article One-o-nine or from the letter of Article Six-o-four."

Nearing the end now, Tolstoy appealed for compassion: "As it makes its choice, the court need only act in the spirit of all our laws, which always tip the scales of justice on the side of mercy, and in the spirit of Article Eighty-one, which, reminding us that judges are also men, says that a court should be more merciful than severe. With this lofty and strict reminder of the law, the accused leaves his fate to the decision of justice."[6]

These were his final words. Tolstoy and Shabunin sat down, and the three judges—Colonel Yunosha, Lieutenant Kolokoltsov, and Ensign Stasyulevich—filed out.

Questions immediately arise. What passed through Tolstoy's mind as he waited in the crowded courtroom surrounded by friendly neighbors such as Bibikov and the hostile landowners he so often referred to contemptuously as "the honorable nobility"?[7] Having spoken "with the most assurance and satisfaction to himself," as he later claimed in a talk with Aylmer Maude, his English biographer, did he think he had saved the soldier's life? Or did he feel he had failed, because, as he told Biryukov, it seemed to him the judges were bored by his plea and listened to him perfunctorily, out of politeness?[8] One cannot say, although it would seem that at that awesome moment he felt he had made the best of a bad situation. Everything now depended on the court and its voting procedure, which was fixed by the regulations. Yunosha had two votes, Kolokoltsov one, Stasyulevich one.[9] Thus if Kolokoltsov and Stasyulevich stuck together, Tolstoy would win, for imposition of the death penalty required three of the four ballots.

And what of Vasili Shabunin, the ugly redhead who as a human being interested no one very much? What mattered to Tolstoy, the aristocrat who so passionately opposed capital punishment, was Shabunin's life, not what happened to him if he were sentenced to prison or exile or a punitive battalion. What mattered to the spectators was how Tolstoy made out, whether he won or lost, not whether Shabunin lived or died.

The judges filed back. Yunosha, flanked by Kolokoltsov and Stasyulevich, announced the finding of the court.

The verdict? Guilty as charged.

The sentence? Death by firing squad.

6

The Anatomy of Power

Tolstoy was a stubborn man, given not to bowing before foregone conclusions but to challenging them, not to resignation but to confrontation. Accordingly, as soon as the sentence was read, he stepped forward. Clearly Yunosha had voted for conviction, and so had one or both of the junior officers. But which was it? If both, the case was finished; Shabunin would die. If only one, Tolstoy had a chance, because a split decision opened the door for an appeal to the tsar, whose autocratic power was indicated by his numerous titles: they occupied nine lines in his ukases and proclamations, and the ninth was followed by a tenth with the words "and so forth, and so forth, and so forth." He soon found out. Grim-faced Stasyulevich had voted for acquittal on the ground of irresponsibility (Article 116), but young Kolokoltsov, who had joined him in urging Tolstoy to take the case, had wavered and in the end sided with his regimental commander.

One would think that at that moment, feeling betrayed, Tolstoy turned livid with anger. There is, however, no evidence to that effect. On the contrary. It has been suggested that Kolokoltsov went along with Yunosha to further his military career, but Tolstoy apparently took the position that he was subjected to more overwhelming pressure, for in later years Kolokoltsov visited his house and he visited Kolokoltsov's, and in his 1908 letter to Biryukov he referred to him as "a kind and good lad." In any event, July 16 was a time for action, not recrimination, and Tolstoy acted swiftly. "Immediately" (*totchas*) after the trial (or so he told Biryukov) he drafted an appeal and sent it with a covering letter to his first cousin once removed, Alexandra Tolstoy, who was also his friend. Alexandra was the daughter of his grandfather's brother, a maid of honor (*freylina*) at court, a tutor of the tsar's children, a force in St. Petersburg society, and an intelligent woman; she would know how to present it. Tolstoy then resumed his daily routine at Yasnaya Polyana, evidently believing the tsar would not reject a petition from a nobleman who had fought for his country and whose family had served Russian sovereigns for generations.

There was a problem, however, and it arose as a consequence of an attempt on the life of the tsar on the fourth day of the preceding April. Tolstoy was aware of the incident, but, living far from the capital and having little interest in politics in those days, he had no reason to expect it would influence Shabunin's fate. The circumstances were these:

After a walk with his daughter in the Summer Garden that morning, the tsar stopped by his carriage to put on his cloak. Suddenly a young man, Dmitri Karakozov, raised a pistol and fired. Almost simultaneously a peasant, Osip Komissarov, who was near Karakozov, uttered some exclamation or struck Karakozov's arm, with the result that the bullet went wild.

Alexander was both frightened and angered. He had liberated the serfs. He had begun to reform the educational and judicial systems. He had other measures in mind. And now they—social revolutionaries—would kill him?

Alexander imagined a widespread conspiracy. He had Karakozov hanged and fired the minister of education because Karakozov had been a student at Kazan University. To

Tolstoy's disgust, he elevated Komissarov to the nobility to demonstrate his gratitude to his peasants and to call attention to their supposed love for him, an act that Tolstoy considered "a stupidity" and "the coup de grace" to the Russian system of class distinctions.[1] The tsar went further. He dismissed the governor general of St. Petersburg, and to conduct an investigation and purge he brought in Count Nikolai Muraviev, who in 1863 had suppressed with exemplary brutality a Polish uprising that had spread to Lithuania. He closed two liberal magazines, *The Contemporary*, which had published Tolstoy's earliest works, and *The Russian Word*, and he exiled to northern Russia and Siberia some known leftists, including the writer Peter Lavrov, a colonel of artillery, a professor of mathematics, and a member of the St. Petersburg municipal council. He initiated other repressive measures, thereby setting an example for his successors, Alexander III and Nicholas II, and perhaps the stage for his own assassination in 1881. As the Russian historian Alexander Kornilov wrote long after: "A stubborn and lasting reaction began in April 1866 and lasted with a few short pauses till [the revolution of] 1905."[2] Thus the mood of the palace and the regime was one of angry determination when Shabunin struck Yasevich. The tsar feared another assassination attempt. His ministers feared acts of terrorism everywhere. His generals feared mass breaches of discipline. In the circumstances, the nearer a man was to the source of power, the more he sought to demonstrate his zealous loyalty to the sovereign. This is, I think, the most plausible explanation for a stunning development that had already taken place when Shabunin was tried and Tolstoy appealed for clemency. As Gusev revealed in 1957, the tsar personally ordered the court-martial.[3] But as the Moscow file on the case makes clear, he evidently did so on the basis of rigged testimony.

Who rigged it? Captain Yasevich? Colonel Yunosha? It is not inconceivable. General Gildenshtubbe in Moscow? General Milyutin in St. Petersburg? It could be. Uncertainty stems from the fact that the file has been tampered with. It is suspiciously incomplete. Yasevich's report to Yunosha is missing. So is Yunosha's to Gildenshtubbe. So is Gildenshtubbe's first report to Milyutin. And so is Gildenshtubbe's order to Yunosha to try the young soldier under Article 604.

The Moscow file opens with Gildenshtubbe's second report to the minister of war. Dated June 15, nine days after the crime, it bears notations that indicate it was received on June 18 and passed on to the judge advocate general three days later:

N 5889   June 18, 1866 [date received]
N 4937   June 21, 1866 [date received]

MOSCOW
MILITARY DISTRICT   TO THE WAR MINISTER.

DISTRICT
STAFF

Judge Advocate's Section
15th of June 1866
No. 5935   REPORT.

MOSCOW   The commander of the 65th Moscow infantry regiment has reported that on the 6th of this June before

[Notation in another hand, dated June 18: "Already reported."] the departure of the 2nd company of the 1st battalion for a battalion exercise, a private of this company, Vasili Shabunin, being in a state of intoxication, did not join the formation, therefore the commander of the company, Staff Captain Yasevich, had him sent to be confined under arrest, but when he, Shabunin, passed by Captian Yasevich, he hit the latter in the face, saying, "Take that [*Ya tebe dam*]."

[Notation in another hand: "New. 1866 N 154."]

I report this matter to Your High Excellency in case you deem it necessary to solicit the Sovereign's consent to turn Private Shabunin over to a military court in accordance with field criminal law.

The Commander in Chief
  Adjutant General Guildenshtubbe

Chief of Staff
  Major General [signature illegible]

It is an intriguing document. The notation to the left of the first paragraph betrays the fact that Milyutin already knew the official version of the incident when he received it—the version that implied that the crime was unprovoked, that there were no extenuating circumstances. The notation to the left of the second paragraph suggests that the only purpose of this report was to set in motion the administrative machinery that eventually would bring the case to the tsar's attention without informing him that Yasevich had thrown Shabunin's paper in his face and later ordered him beaten with birch rods.

Now, one may ask whether there is any possibility that the official version was correct, and the answer to that question has to be: only if one is prepared to believe that Stasyulevich and Kolokoltsov lied to or misinformed Tolstoy when they asked him to defend Shabunin, and then only if the court sat silent while Tolstoy gave a false version of the incident to three officer acquaintances who certainly were familiar with the circumstances of the case. In any event, the accuracy of Tolstoy's version is supported by the fact that he gave a copy of his plea to the Tula newspaper while the army concealed its version in a classified file that has not been revealed until now.

Milyutin sent Gildenshtubbe's second report to the judge advocate general, and the judge advocate general replied on June 21 in the same vein, as the second document in the Moscow file discloses:

N 267   June 24, 1866 [date received]

WAR MINISTRY
Judge Advocate's Department

A significant breech of military discipline by Private Shabunin

Ordered by the Sovereign to be judged according to field military regulations.

      Ad. Gen. Milyutin
      June 25, 1866

1866 N 154

The commander of the 65th Moscow infantry regiment has reported to the Commander in Chief of the Moscow Military District that on the 6th of this June, before the departure of the 2nd company of the 1st battalion of the aforesaid regiment for a battalion exercise, a private of this company, Vasili Shabunin, being in a state of intoxication, did not join the formation and therefore was sent to be confined under arrest by the company commander, Staff Captain Yasevich, but when Shabunin passed by Staff Captain Yasevich he struck the latter in the face, saying, "Take that."

Adjutant General Gildenshtubbe informs Your High Excellency of this matter in case you deem it necessary to ask for the Sovereign's consent to turn over Private Shabunin to a military court in accordance with field criminal law.

The Law

Point 6 in the note to Article 17 of Volume 1 of the Milit[ary] Crimin[al] Code [further identification of reference unclear].

Running the gauntlet or punishment by *shpitsruten* [a word of German origin meaning the same thing] has been canceled completely for lower military ranks in peacetime as in wartime; along with this softening of punishment in ordinary cases, the accused in significant breaches of discipline and public security which call for more severe and immediate punishment are to be brought to trial in accordance with field military law not only in wartime but also in peacetime, and assigned the punishments prescribed for wartime. Such action is to be car-carried out with the consent of the Sovereign or by order of the commanders in chief or other high military authorities vested with equal powers.

Conclusion

The Judge Advocate's Department has the honor to communicate this presentation of Adjutant General Gildenshtubbe for Your High Excellency's consideration in case it is deemed desirable to seek the Sovereign's permission to continue this case, and in the event that His Majesty deigns to turn Private Shabunin over to a field military court, to delegate the right of final ratification

of [the verdict in] this affair to the
Commander in Chief of the Moscow
Military District.

Judge Advocate General Filosofof

No. 3589
June 21, 1866

Director of the Office [signature illegible]

The plot thickens. Gildenshtubbe suggests (June 15) that the case be taken to the tsar. Filosofof suggests (June 21) that the tsar give Gildenshtubbe the right to ratify or confirm whatever sentence a court-martial imposes. And Milyutin, at the seat of power, appears to propose nothing on his own. He receives Filosofof's report on June 24 and the next day, in the role of a concerned but personally uninvolved minister of war, takes it to the palace. There, as his notation to the left of Filosofof's report indicates, he wins the tsar's consent to proceed as desired against Shabunin. The tsar's consent is conveyed to Gildenshtubbe in another report, which constitutes the third document in the Moscow file. Unlike the first two, which are originals and, as such, model examples of the calligrapher's art, it is a rough copy:

To the Commander in Chief of the
Moscow Military District

Office
Desk 2
June 25, 1866
N 3680
Answer to N 5935

His Majesty the Emperor Sovereignly deigns to order that a private of the 65th Moscow infantry regiment, Vasili Shabunin, [who is] guilty of a significant breach of military discipline, be turned over to a military court in accordance with field military law, and that the right of final

	ratification be delegated to Your High Excellency.
Signed:	W[ar] Minister
	Adjutant Gen. Milyutin
Countersigned:	Judge Advocate General Filosofof
True copy:	Secretary Groshev

No. 154

It was all smoothly, sinuously done. There is no mention of the death penalty in these first three documents in the Moscow file, or in any of the others that survive, but Gildenshtubbe now ordered that Shabunin be tried under Article 604, and Article 604, as we have seen, was unequivocal: "Raising a hand or weapon against a superior is to be punished by death."

Yunosha did as he was told, though it seems with some reluctance, for along with himself he appointed Tolstoy's riding companions, Stasyulevich and Kolokoltsov, as officers of the court, and he had no objection to Tolstoy's participation as counsel for the defense. One imagines that at the trial on July 16 the special prosecutor from Moscow, concentrating on the crime itself, kept silent about the official version of the circumstances that led up to it, and that, acting as if they were irrelevant, he said nothing when Tolstoy told his version of what happened inside the *izba*. Be that as it may, when Tolstoy appealed to the tsar, he was unaware of Gildenshtubbe's report to Milyutin and Milyutin's background part in the affair. In sum, before, during, and after the trial he was just another fly in another web of bureaucratic power and intrigue, a count and former lieutenant of artillery who, though loyal to the regime, had no idea what was going on in the upper reaches of the army, an aristocrat who was no more influential in the case than the peasants in the villages around Yasnaya Polyana. When the trial ended, they gathered before the brick *izba* at Ozerki where Shabunin once again was confined, this time in leg irons with the right half of his head shaved, a *smertnik*, one condemned to death. They asked to see and console the prisoner. Permission denied. They sought to leave gifts for the condemned man. Permission granted. Some donated an egg or two, others a little milk. It was always so in the great Russian countryside, where the masses sympathized with anyone, guilty or not, who became entangled in the sticky net of the law.

As for Tolstoy, in the two weeks following the trial he was busy as usual at Yasnaya Polyana, apparently giving little thought to his petition, which he was convinced was in good hands. He continued to supervise the construction of a small addition to his house, which would give him a study on the ground floor—away from the children—where he could write undisturbed. He paid off some loans and worked with a steward he had taken on to manage the estate, thanks to 2,306.25 rubles (about $1,150.00) that had just come in from the serialization of the second part of his novel, and he undoubtedly gave some thought to the scope of that work, which he now proposed to rewrite and expand for book publication. Sonya's diary seems to indicate that something else was on his mind. Something else was surely on hers. On July 19 she wrote:

We've got a new factor for the estate. His wife is young, good-looking, and a *nihilist*. She and Lyova [Leo] have long, lively talks on literature and politics. I find these talks rather out of place—flattering to her, and painful to me. He used to preach that an outsider, especially a young and attractive person, ought not to be admitted into the intimate family circle—and yet in practice he always does the opposite. Of course, I don't show any sign of being displeased, although I haven't a moment of peace now. Since Ilya's birth [their third child and second son, born May 22] we have been sleeping in separate rooms, which is wrong; for if we were together I wouldn't stand it any longer, but would blurt it all out to him this very evening; but I can't go to him now,—and it is the same with him. My children make me very happy; they give me so much joy that it seems a sin to ask for more. There is so much happiness in loving them; but it is a pity that Lyova should break his own rules. Yet why did he say today that a husband would be afraid to hurt a wife, whose conduct was irreproachable? As if one were only unhappy after one's husband had already *done* something evil. It's a great misfortune if for a second one's husband doubts in his soul that he loves his wife. Lyova is wrong to treat Marya Ivanova [the new factor's wife] to such grand speeches. It is nearly 1 o'clock, but I can't sleep. I just feel as if that nihilist woman were going to be my bête noire.[4]

July 22:

This morning Lyova made some excuse for going to that house [the Tolstoy family's term for the other wing of the dismantled mansion, where the steward and his wife lived]. So M. I. [Marya Ivanova] told me, and she also said that he had talked to her below the balcony. What was the need of going there in the rain? It's quite obvious that he likes her, and the thought of it drives me insane. I wish her every misfortune, but to her face, for some reason, I am particularly pleasant. I wonder how soon her husband will turn out to be useless, so that they can both go away? But, in the meantime, this jealousy will kill me. He is extremely cold to me. My breasts are very sore, and it is real agony to nurse the child. I called in Marfusha [Marya Afanasyev, the old family nurse] today, and made her feed the child, so that my breasts might have a rest. My suffering always seems to make him treat me badly; he always grows cold, and that adds mental agony to my physical pain. I remain locked up in my own room, while she sits in the drawing room with the children. I simply can't bear her; it always annoys me to see her beauty and vivaciousness, especially when Lyova is there.[5]

July 24:

Lyova went again to that house, and said afterward that the poor woman found life very dull. Then he asked me why I hadn't invited them to dinner. If only I could forbid her ever to come into the house at all, I would gladly do it. My dear Lyova! Can't you see how easily you get caught! The pain in my breast takes up much of my time and happiness. The worst of it is that Lyova and I have become strangers to one another. I got Marfusha to nurse Ilyusha [Ilya], who is rather restless; and it makes me sad to see him suck somebody else's breast. Goodness only knows when my breasts will heal; everything seems to be all wrong. My heart leaps with joy when I see Lyova dissatisfied with the farm work. Maybe he'll dismiss the factor, and then I'll get rid of this dreadful feeling of jealousy. I'd be sorry for him, but I cannot bear her.[6]

Still no word from St. Petersburg, but Tolstoy cannot have been surprised, for in the summer of 1866 a letter took four or five days to get there from Yasnaya Polyana (by coach or horseman to Moscow and by train from Moscow to St. Petersburg), and Tolstoy knew it would take a day or two for Alexandra to see Milyutin, the minister of war, a day or two for Milyutin to call the appeal to the tsar's attention, and another day or so, whatever the tsar pleased, for the tsar to act upon it. Even so, he had reason to hope for an answer by the end of the month or the first week in August. It is therefore surprising that on July 25, nine days after the trial, he planned a trip away from home. On that day he wrote to his friend Afanasi Fet, who lived some distance to the south, saying he expected to arrive between July 28 and August 3 at the estate of a mutual friend, Nikolai Kireyevsky, where the hunting was excellent. He suggested that Fet meet him there, adding that if Fet could not make it, he would stop at Fet's place on the way back.[7]

Tolstoy never made that trip, apparently because some days later he received a devastating letter from St. Petersburg in the handwriting of Alexandra. She had received Tolstoy's petition. She had seen Milyutin. There was, however, a hitch. Tolstoy, she said, had neglected to include the number of Shabunin's regiment, and Milyutin was taking the position that he could not send an incomplete dossier to the palace.

Consternation! If Milyutin didn't know already, he could have found out from the Moscow Military District, which had jurisdiction over the case.

Tolstoy quickly corrected his mistake, or so he later claimed. Biryukov says he sent a telegram, and perhaps he did, though one cannot be certain. Tolstoy's first letter to Alexandra, her reply to him, and his telegram or second letter to her (whichever it was) are missing along with some other documents that relate to the Shabunin affair. Besides, as his letter to Fet indicates, he began to act very oddly about this time, unlike a responsible counsel for the defense with a passionate sense of mission or a determined, vigorous foe of the death penalty. At the end of July or early in August, a day or two before or after hearing from Alexandra, he wrote to his brother Sergei and again said he was leaving home, this time for Nikolskoye, the estate he inherited from his brother Nikolai. He asked Sergei for a loan of 200 rubles (about $100), saying he had made a "stupid mistake" in hiring a factor to manage Yasnaya Polyana for 30 rubles (about $15) a month.[8]

At such a critical moment for Shabunin? While Tolstoy

was awaiting an answer from Alexandra or Milyutin or the tsar? From now on the record tells a strange and terrible story.

On July 25, the day Tolstoy wrote to Fet and almost certainly a day or two after Alexandra saw Milyutin, the minister of war was concerned. He could not send Tolstoy's appeal to the palace, for it would reveal to the tsar that there were two versions of the incident, and the tsar, feeling he had been misinformed, might set aside the verdict under circumstances that could affect Milyutin's career adversely. Better get on with the case. Had Gildenshtubbe ratified the death sentence? Impatiently Milyutin wrote an urgent note in his own hand to the judge advocate general.

Needed

I request information in connection with the affair concerning a private of the Moscow or Butirski inf. regt. (I do not remember for sure which one), who struck his company commander in the face. In June of this year this private was turned over for trial according to field laws. The sentence was submitted to Adj. Gen. Gildenshtubbe for ratification.

How did he ratify it?

D. Milyutin

July 25

The letter suggests the cunning ways of the minister of war. He did not mention Shabunin's name. He could not recall to which regiment he was attached. And the question he asked was so ambiguously worded (*"V chëm sostayala konfirmatsiya yego?"*—literally, "What did his ratification consist of?") that it could be taken to mean he wanted to know not what action Gildenshtubbe had taken but what form it took. In fact, Gildenshtubbe had not yet acted, as the fifth and sixth documents in the Moscow file make apparent. The fifth is in answer to Milyutin's question:

N 6064   July 28, 1866 [date received]

Following the order of Your High Excellency and enclosing herewith the original report concerning Private Shabunin of the *Moscow* regiment, who, according to field law, was brought to trial for having struck his company commander, I have the honor to inform you that after a most careful search no information about the ratification of this affair by Adjutant General Gildenshtubbe has been received by the Judge Advocate's Department.

In any event I consider it my duty to enclose herewith a report in which the Sovereign was notified of a ratification by the Commander in Chief of the Moscow Military District, which occurred in May of this year in the case of Privates Ivanov and Golomoin, who were prosecuted for a similar crime.

Acting Judge Advocate General [signature illegible]
July 26, 1866

A week later Gildenshtubbe took the action Milyutin was waiting for, as Milyutin found out on August 6 through the sixth document in the Moscow file:

	August 6, 1866 [date received]
No. 6349	August 8, 1866 [date received]
MOSCOW	
MILITARY DISTRICT	TO THE WAR MINISTER

DISTRICT
STAFF

Judge Advocate's Section
August 2, 1866   REPORT.
No. 7757   In reference to 442.831 and 832, Vol. 2, of the Military Criminal
MOSCOW   Code, I have the honor to present to Your High Excellency for use in

Some Call It Murder

a most respectful report to His Majesty the Emperor a copy of my ratification [of the verdict] in connection with the court-martial of Private Vasili Shabunin of the 65th Moscow infantry regiment.

The Commander in Chief
Adjutant General Gildenshtubbe

Chief of Staff
Major General [signature illegible]

Gildenshtubbe's ratification report and the text of the order he sent to Colonel Yunosha are missing, but the consequences are clear as noonday. On the morning of August 9, a Tuesday, the Second Company of the Sixty-fifth Regiment, Captain Yasevich in command, marched behind the regimental band to a field near the settlement of Novaya Kolpna, about a mile from Yasenki. With it were men from other companies who were being disciplined for one offense or another. Awaiting it were Colonel Yunosha and members of his staff.

In that field a stake, painted black, had been driven into the ground. Behind it a pit had been dug.

While peasants who lived or worked nearby looked on, the troops formed a square into which Shabunin, accompanied by a black-clad priest, was led. It is said he walked with unfaltering step, head up, eyes downcast, that the sentence of death was read out, that he kissed a cross the priest extended to him, that they dressed him in a "shroud" (a white shirt), tied his hands behind his back, blindfolded him, strapped him to the stake.

At a command, twelve sharpshooters ran out from their scattered places in the ranks. They lined up fifteen paces from Shabunin and fired. Two shots hit him in the head, four in the heart.[9] As the torn body sagged against the straps, a doctor stepped forward to make sure he was dead.

All according to regulations. A priest was there because in a Christian country it was unthinkable for the state to kill a man without benefit of clergy. A doctor was there because only someone trained to sustain life was authorized to certify its passing.

And where was the counsel for the defense when the shots rang out? Where was Leo Tolstoy?

Standing right there where he should have been, says Biryukov: "One can imagine what went on in the soul of Leo Nikolayevich at the sight of this atrocity that was committed before his eyes."[10] *Pravo* says "perhaps" he was present, suggesting that the Tula paper's account from which it got its information was unclear on the point.[11]

Shabunin's limp body was released from the stake and thrown into the pit behind it. Several men shoveled in the dirt. The sharpshooters ran back to their units. Then, with band playing, Colonel Yunosha leading the way, the troops marched past the grave and left the field.

Justice had been done, and the men of the Sixty-fifth now knew for sure what happened to a soldier who "raised a hand" against a superior. Milyutin, the minister of war, saw to that. He could have ordered his own investigation of the incident and did not. He could have passed on Tolstoy's appeal to the tsar and did not. But he went further. The seventh and last of the substantial documents in the Moscow file indicates that he concealed from the tsar Gildenshtubbe's ratification or approval of the death sentence until two days after the execution, as if he feared for reasons best known to himself that the tsar might intervene at the last moment. It is a memorandum dated August 12, and as a notation to the left of the document explains, it was an answer to Gildenshtubbe's report (N. 7757) dated August 2, a week before Shabunin died:

6462

WAR MINISTRY	To the Commander in Chief of the Moscow Military District.

Judge Advocate's
Department

Section
Judge Advocate General
Desk 1
August 12, 1866
No. 4704
Answer to N. 7757 about
note of ratification to the
Sovereign

Ratification by Your High Excellency [of the verdict] concerning the private of the 65th Moscow infantry regiment. Shabunin, was reported on the 11th of this August to His Majesty the Emperor.—Signed: The War Minister, Adjutant General Milyutin. Countersigned: Judge Advocate General Filosofof.

True copy: Judge Advocate [signature illegible]

This memorandum tied up the loose administrative ends at the war ministry, and Milyutin could close the file with feelings of satisfaction. Thanks to him, the tsar was still on his throne and all was well with St. Petersburg. The death penalty, however, has a life of its own. For Shabunin, the young redhead who bloodied the nose of his superior, the ordeal was over, but for Leo Tolstoy, the aristocrat who tried to save him, it was just beginning. Whether he understood this or not I cannot say. Probably not, for he left home the morning after Shabunin's riddled body was dumped in the pit and went hunting for five days.

7

Strange Behavior

The horrified peasants of Yasenki, Ozerki, and Novaya Kolpna reacted instinctively, impulsively, to the execution of Private Shabunin. As soon as the troops marched from the field, they rushed toward the pile of freshly turned earth that concealed the still-warm body and stood about, wailing and making the sign of the cross, with the thumb of the right hand touching the first two fingers, the hand moving from brow to breast, then to the right, then to the left, in the manner of the Russian Orthodox church. Others joined them when the day's work was done, and soon a village priest arrived to recite the office of the dead. Candles were lighted and thrown on the grave along with symbolic pieces of cloth and copper coins. Some women shrieked, others fainted. Men knelt and touched their foreheads to the ground. Fearing a demonstration, officials sent for district policemen. Sentries were posted to hold back the ragged crowd, and the burial mound was leveled in the vain hope that the peasants would forget where it was and it would not become a place of pilgrimage and silent protest.[1]

And Leo Tolstoy? Did he stay behind with the peasants or ride away when the execution was over? Indeed, from the entry in Sonya's diary the next day, one may ask whether he was ever there, Biryukov's testimony to the contrary. On August 10 Sonya wrote:

> There are days when I feel so happy and cheerful that I long to do something that would make everybody love and admire me. In contrast to the misfortunes of which I have heard, I feel particularly happy. Bibikov told us a terrible story yesterday, about a regimental clerk in Yasenki who was shot for hitting his lieutenant in the face. Lyova defended him at the open court-martial, but, unfortunately, the defense was a purely formal affair.

So, if one may believe Sonya (and there is no reason not to), it was Bibikov and not her husband who told her of Shabunin's death—told "us" about Shabunin's death. Meaning herself and her house guests at the time or herself and Leo? Whatever she meant, it would seem that if he did attend the execution, he did not speak of it when he got home, which suggests that, however he felt about his plea to the court, however pained he was by his failure to include the name of the regiment in his appeal to the tsar, he was determined at this stage not to accept responsibility for what happened: he would live his life from then on as if Shabunin had never lived. One cannot be certain. There is no known Tolstoy diary for the years 1865–78. No surviving letter or recorded conversation explains his thinking in the matter. But one may speculate from his behavior in the days, weeks, and months to come that his reasoning went something like this: Shabunin *had* struck Captain Yasevich; he *had* refused to participate in his own defense; he, Tolstoy, had done what he could to save him; and although he failed, he was not going to let that failure destroy him. Some such line of thought would explain why he went hunting the next day, carefree, it would appear, writing home in his absence letters in which he never mentioned the case. Sonya's diary

Strange Behavior

entry for August 10, the day after the execution and the day Tolstoy left home, continues:

> We have lots of visitors; the Gorchakov princesses, Prince Lvov [from Tula], a very nice man, and that fat fellow [Vladimir] Sollogub [a writer], with his two sons. He said that I was the ideal "author's wife"—one who would know how to nurse *her husband's talent*; I am grateful to him for saying it, and shall do my best to be even more of a nurse for Lyova's talent. My jealousy about M. I. has completely gone—there was really nothing in it. My relations with Lyova are good and pleasant, though still a little cold. My children are such darlings. Seryozha [Sergei, their oldest child] started calling me *thou* today. I am sorry to find that he has forgotten his alphabet during the summer; last winter he knew it so well.[2]

Altogether an intriguing entry, given its brief reference to Shabunin and the fact it contains no indication whether Tolstoy attended the execution or how it affected him or even that he left home that morning, taking with him his coachman, Kuzma, and an old horse he planned to return to his friend Dmitri Dyakov when he passed by Cheremoshnya, to the south. Tolstoy headed toward Chern and Mtsensk and that night wrote a letter to Sonya from Lapotkovo, a village about fifteen miles from Yasnaya Polyana: "I am sending you five snipe. I did not get as far as Fominka; all were shot near Karamishevo [in a swamp where Tolstoy often hunted]. Eat, remember me, and wait for my return. I shall arrive probably on my own [horses]. Give twenty kopecks [ten cents] to the bearer of the snipe."[3]

Not a word about the execution, either then or in the letters that followed. The next day he wrote Sonya:

> I got as far as Sergievskoye at two o'clock this morning. And slept beautifully in the hay. Did you receive the snipe

and note from Lapotkovo? I am spending the night and drinking tea at the *izba* of a dear little Russian peasant. What a pig and sloven. Dyakov's horse is so weak that not only must I abandon her but I am afraid Kuzma will take home only the hide and collar. Her death is not going to be on my conscience—I have been traveling very slowly. I kiss you, darling, little aunt, and the children.[4]

A dead horse on his conscience would have been too much. On August 12 he wrote:

Driving a team [of horses], I arrived at Chern at two o'clock. Saw how Dyakov's [horse] staggered and almost died. What a terrible pity.

Have just met an old hussar officer. A Vaska Denisov of our time—bad. [An apparent reference to Vasili Denisov, first introduced in *War and Peace* as Nikolai Rostov's squadron commander in the Pavlograd Hussars.] A hussar with a touch of nihilism. [As the term was first used by Turgenev, a nihilist was "a man who would accept no authority and adopt no principle as an article of faith."] Am staying tonight at Masha's [Tolstoy's younger sister, Marya, who had moved from Pirogovo to an estate at Pokrovskoye, four or five miles from Chern]; tomorrow, with God's favor, I go early to Nikolskoye and on to Dyakov's [ten or eleven miles from Nikolskoye] for breakfast.

I shall pass the night there; but in any case will not be home before Monday [August 15].

Farewell, my dear. I kiss you and the children.[5]

Three letters home, all written as if there had been no Shabunin affair or as if he had nothing to say about it to Sonya or they had agreed to speak of it no more. "One must not submit to the past," Levin's inner voice tells him in *Anna Karenina,* and such may have been Tolstoy's determination at the time, although several other explanations for his silence are possible. Class outlook, for one. Shabunin was a *meshchanin,* Tolstoy a count in a family whose members had been counts and countesses since the early eighteenth century. For another, however difficult it is to believe, he may have been so engrossed in thoughts of his novel while he prowled the fields and swamps in search of game that the execution was far from his mind. Some writers are like that. They may appear to be interested in an engaging conversation or some other distraction, but the story they are trying to write is never far from their consciousness. If it fades, it comes back, presses itself upon them, insists on being considered to the exclusion of all else. One must judge from the available record, however, and the record indicates that, perhaps because of the Shabunin affair, Tolstoy had trouble getting down to work when he returned home. In May he had written to his friend Fet saying he hoped to finish his novel by the end of the year and to publish it in book form with illustrations by the artist Mikhail Bashilov.[6] In late June he confirmed to Bashilov his expectation that he would finish it that year "without fail," and said he now wanted sixty illustrations instead of the thirty previously ordered.[7] But he accomplished little in July at the time of the trial, in early August at the time of the execution, or later when the August 21 issue of the Tula paper published its version of the incident, which was similar to Tolstoy's and unlike that of the high command of the army. And in September he turned his attention to other matters. He wrote a play called *The Nihilist* (very short, to be produced at Yasnaya Polyana by members of the family and friends) and planned a dinner and dance for the seventeenth, his wife's name day.

As he looked forward to that evening, the names of the guests he would invite came quickly to his mind: his sister-in-law Tanya Bers, the Dyakovs, their two daughters and the daughters' governess, his sister, Marya, and her two daughters.

Almost all women, and one needs men for a dance. Tolstoy had a solution to that problem. He'd ask Colonel Yunosha, Kolokoltsov, and Stasyulevich.

And what about an orchestra? He'd get musicians from the regimental band that had played at the execution.

The story comes from Tanya's memoirs, *Tolstoy as I Knew Him*, in which she writes she "often" went riding with Yunosha, Kolokoltsov ("an old acquaintance"), and Stasyulevich ("whose gloomy countenance astounded me"). Tanya wrote:

> The seventeenth of September arrived. Everyone was in a holiday mood. We were all elegantly dressed in light white dresses with colored ribbons. The dinner table was decorated with flowers and the new terrace [the porch above Tolstoy's study in the new addition to the house] was flooded with sunshine. I remember how gaily and noisily we sat down to dinner at five o'clock in the afternoon [the usual hour in the Tolstoy household], when suddenly an orchestra started to play in the garden. It was the overture from the opera *Fenella ou La Muette de Portici* [by Auber], which Sonya so loved. All of us, except Sonya, knew that Leo Nikolayevich had asked Colonel Yunosha to send the orchestra, but the secret was well kept.[8]

Yunosha and his two junior officers arrived after dinner, and the dance was organized. "All this took place on the terrace," writes Tanya. "Stasyulevich danced only the quadrille, upon compulsion."

Stasyulevich was not the only reluctant dancer. When the orchestra played the Kamarinskaya, a folk dance, no one took to the floor. Tolstoy called for volunteers. No one volunteered. He turned to Kolokoltsov. "Go ahead, dance," he shouted. "Surely, you cannot hold out." The orchestra played louder and louder. "Come now! Eh?" Tolstoy urged, and Kolokoltsov stepped forward and danced with Tanya while the others clapped their hands to the beat.

Tanya recalls "the beauty and warmth" of the night: "We

all went down the decorative [outdoor] stairway to the garden avenue. The moon was on the wane and would rise only around eleven o'clock. After the dances, the musicians were treated to supper and beer, and at one o'clock in the morning they set out with the officers for Yasenki, playing a march."

What an extraordinary sight! Yunosha, Kolokoltsov, and Stasyulevich riding on ahead, the band following on foot, and Leo Tolstoy, with what thoughts one can only imagine, standing in the garden watching them disappear in the moonlight.

Almost two months later, on November 12, Sonya told her diary of the same evening. To her, as to her nineteen-year-old sister, it had been a happy occasion:

It gives me great joy to think of my name-day, when at dinner, much to my pleasant surprise, the band began to play. I remember the affectionate look in Leo's eyes during the day, and the evening we spent on the verandah, which was lit up with Chinese lanterns, and I can still see the gay young girls in their white muslin dresses, and that genial little fellow Kolokoltsov and, above all, my beloved Lyova, looking so lively and excited, and doing his best to make us as happy as possible. I was surprised that such a sedate and solemn matron as myself [Sonya was twenty-two years old on August 22, Tolstoy thirty-eight on August 28] could dance with so much gusto. The weather was glorious, and everything was lovely.[9]

"Everything was lovely"—and yet it is not far-fetched, I think, to suggest that already, deep in the recesses of Tolstoy's soul, the seed of an idea was germinating which would emerge as a consequence of the Shabunin affair and find expression in the horror of the execution scene in *War and Peace* and in Pierre's reaction to the sight of five Russians dying before a French firing squad:

From the moment Pierre had witnessed those terrible murders committed by men who did not wish to commit them, it was as if the mainspring of his life, on which everything depended and which made everything appear alive, had suddenly been wrenched out and everything had collapsed into a heap of meaningless rubbish. Though he did not acknowledge it to himself, his faith in the right ordering of the universe, in humanity, in his own soul, and in God, had been destroyed. He had experienced this before, but never so strongly as now. When similar doubts had assailed him before, they had been the result of his own wrong doing, and at the bottom of his heart he had felt that relief from his despair and from those doubts was to be found within himself. But now he felt that the universe had crumbled before his eyes and only meaningless ruins remained, and this was not by any fault of his own. He felt that it was not in his power to regain faith in the meaning of life.[10]

Tolstoy's early reaction to Shabunin's death was quite different from Pierre's in *War and Peace*. His departure on a hunting trip the following day, the banal letters he wrote home during his absence, and the way he celebrated Sonya's name day suggest cold indifference, a shrug of the shoulders. One may believe, however, that his conscience, whether inactive or subdued by an effort of will, was alert and biding its time. Little as he cared to think of it, he had made a mistake in his appeal to the tsar.

PART TWO

The Enigmatic Years

I only know two very real evils in life: remorse and illness. The only good is the absence of those evils. To live for myself avoiding those two evils is my whole philosophy now.

—Prince Andrei in *War and Peace*

The main thing, so far as I'm concerned, is not to feel guilty.

—Levin in *Anna Karenina*

8

Back to *War and Peace*

After the observance of Sonya's name day and the presentation at home of *The Nihilist*, Tolstoy returned to his novel with a clearer understanding of where he was going and how he proposed to get there. Not counting the play, which ran to only fourteen pages or so and which exists only in a revised form as *A Comedy in Three Acts*, he had written little in May, June, July, August, and September, but by early October he was determined to carry his story to and beyond Napoleon's invasion of Russia in 1812 and to build it around a new philosophy of history, the theme of which would be that outstanding individuals— emperors, kings, cabinet ministers, field marshals, generals, and the like—do not direct and control the stream of history, but are swept along by some mysterious, collective human current, like everyone else. (The idea did not originate with him, but he warmly embraced it now.) More eager than ever to bring out his novel in book form, he was also determined to change the title from *The Year 1805*—not to *All's Well That Ends Well*, as he had told his friend Fet in the spring, but to *War and Peace*. So far, all he had to show for his work besides the chapters that had appeared in *The Russian Herald* were two reprints, one of 167 pages that came out in 1865 and another that included the first part and the second, of 130 pages, subtitled "War," which had appeared in the spring of 1866. It was then with book in mind, letting the Shabunin affair simmer beneath the surface of his mind, that Tolstoy reached for the pen. He wrote rapidly and by November 10 was far enough advanced to leave for Moscow, where he conferred with his editor, Mikhail Katkov, and the artist Bashilov. They talked of continuing the magazine serialization and bringing out everything in an ambitious series of volumes, and it was apparently at this time that he revealed his new title, for less than two months later, on January 6, 1867, the following news item was published in *East,* an Astrakhan weekly, which Gusev attributes to a leak from Katkov:

> Count L. N. Tolstoy has finished half his novel, which has been appearing in *The Russian Herald* under the title *The Year 1805.* At the present time the author has brought his tale to the year 1807 and the peace of Tilsit [signed by Napoleon and Alexander I on a raft in the Niemen River]. The first part, which is already known to the readers of *The Russian Herald,* has been changed significantly by the author, and the entire novel will be coming out under the title *War and Peace* in an independent edition of four volumes with magnificent illustrations, no sooner, however, than the end of the current year.[1]

Tolstoy was not so far along as this release indicated, but with the long summer behind him he returned to Yasnaya Polyana on November 19 (taking the train as far as Serpukhov on the only completed section of the new rail line) and from then on wrote feverishly and kept at it for months. He revised much of what he had written, broke new ground, and in the spring, dissatisfied with Bashilov and having come to believe (with Sonya) that serialization was not the way to handle an epic of such proportions, dropped Katkov and signed a contract with another printer for four volumes (later six) without illustrations, which he would finance himself.

Everything was now *War and Peace,* and everything was going well, but then a striking development occurred that might have slowed Tolstoy down. Alexander Stasyulevich, the gloomy ensign he had known in the Caucasus and the only judge to vote for acquittal, committed suicide.

The reason is not clear. The Shabunin affair lifted Stasyulevich from the obscurity of history and dropped him, and I know of no published speculation about his motive for suicide. It may be that having been forced to serve as a private in the ranks, he could not stand being an ensign in a regiment commanded by his former classmate; or that having voted for acquittal against the will of Yunosha and the minister of war and the tsar, he was subjected to further humiliation; or that Shabunin's execution was more than he could bear. All we know is that sometime in the summer of 1867, a year after the shots were fired in the field near Yasnaya Polyana, after the regiment had moved to another district, Stasyulevich, who could not swim, put on a heavy coat and drowned himself in a river.

"This," says Tanya without mentioning the Shabunin case, "was a great shock to Leo Nikolayevich, who recalled it long afterward with amazement at such strength of will."[2]

How much of a shock? Not one, I think, he could not handle, for although compassionate by nature and a man who liked to be liked, Tolstoy kept his distance from others. There was a suggestion of aloofness about him that discouraged intimacy or affection in his personal relationships with other men, and it evidently manifested itself in his association with Stasyulevich. One would think he had a warm spot in his heart for this soldier he had met in the Caucasus in 1853, drawn upon for his story *Meeting a Moscow Acquaintance in the Detachment,* and known again at Yasnaya Polyana. One would think Stasyulevich made a strong and favorable

impression on him during Shabunin's trial and at his execution. But such, it appears, was not the case. In his 1908 letter
to Biryukov he described him as "ambitious and proud,"
one who evoked "a mixed feeling of compassion and respect," and with whom contact was "pleasant." No more.
And along about the same time he sent a mystifying letter to
Stasyulevich's older brother Mikhail, the distinguished editor of *The European Herald,* whom he had met in Paris in
1857 (he recorded the meeting in his diary on Feburary 21 of
that year). After 1857 Tolstoy and Mikhail exchanged a few
letters and saw each other at least once, in St. Petersburg in
1880, but in 1908 he wrote as if he had scarcely known
Alexander, as if he had never told Mikhail he knew him at
all. He got Alexander's name wrong, called him Matvei, and
suggested that his only contact with him was during the
Shabunin affair. "What kind of man was your brother?" Tolstoy asked, as if he did not know. "Why was he reduced to
the ranks?" as if he did not know.[3]

Tanya is more explicit about her own reaction to the suicide. The only member of the family other than Tolstoy to
mention it in writing, she says: "For a long time I remembered that desolate expression of the young man's eyes [he
was twice her age in 1866]; I never saw him smile, and I was
angry with myself for not having asked him why he was like
that, and for not showing more sympathy for him. Perhaps
it would have made things easier for him, if only while he
was at Yasnaya."[4]

There is no such recorded comment from Tolstoy, who
soon got over "the great shock," if great shock it was, for he
published his first three volumes in January 1868, the fourth
in March of that year, the fifth a year later, and the sixth
and last in December 1869. During this period of extraordinary creative labor he seems to have been more or less satisfied with himself and his way of life. It is my notion,
however, that from time to time an inner voice spoke to him

reproachfully, accusingly, and that Tolstoy talked back, fortified by his new conception of history, which minimized the role of personal responsibility, and perhaps by the consoling thought that he was making amends in his writing for whatever mistakes he had made in his plea to the military court and his appeal to the tsar. Although he knew nothing about the army's classified version of the incident, in the last half and especially in the last third of his novel he turned savagely on the army, war, courts-martial, executions, and the church.[5]

Pierre thinking: "We all profess the Christian law of forgiveness of injuries and love of our neighbors, the law in honor of which we have built in Moscow forty times forty churches—but yesterday a deserter was knouted to death and a minister of that same law of love and forgiveness, a priest, gave the soldier a cross to kiss before his execution" (p. 594).

Prince Andrei to Pierre before Borodino: War "is the most horrible thing in life." And in the next paragraph: "The aim of war is murder; the methods of war are spying, treachery, and their encouragement, the ruin of a country's inhabitants, robbing them or stealing to provision the army, and fraud and falsehood termed military craft. The habits of the military class are the absence of freedom, that is, discipline, idleness, ignorance, cruelty, debauchery, and drunkenness" (p. 865).

After Vereshchagin is torn to pieces by a Moscow mob: "The thought which tranquilized Rostopchin was not a new one. Since the world began and men have killed one another no one has ever committed such a crime against his fellow man without comforting himself with this same idea. This idea is *le bien public*, the hypothetical welfare of other people" (p. 993).

Pierre is being questioned by three officers of a French military court:

These questions, like questions put at trials generally, left the essence of the matter aside, shut out the possibility of that essence's being revealed, and were designed only to form a channel through which the judges wished the answers of the accused to flow so as to lead to the desired result, namely a conviction. . . . He knew he was in these men's power, that only by force had they brought him there, that force alone gave them the right to demand answers to their questions, and that the sole object of that assembly was to inculpate him. [P. 1064]

There follows Tolstoy's horrifyingly vivid account of the execution of five Russians by a French firing squad. Then:

Those dreadful moments [Pierre] had lived through at the executions had as it were forever washed away from his imagination and memory the agitating thoughts and feelings that had formerly seemed so important. [P. 1122]

In the corporal's changed face, in the sound of his voice, in the stirring and deafening noise of the drums, he recognized that mysterious, callous force which compelled people against their will to kill their fellow men—that force the effect of which he had witnessed during the executions. [P. 1125]

Pierre felt that that fatal force which had crushed him during the executions, but which he had not felt during his imprisonment, now again controlled his existence. [P. 1129]

[After Karatayev is shot:] Two French soldiers ran past Pierre, one of whom carried a lowered and smoking gun. They both looked pale, and in the expression on their faces—one of them glanced timidly at Pierre—there was something resembling what he had seen on the face of the young soldier at the execution. [P. 1181]

Back to *War and Peace*

[Pierre telling Natasha about the death of Karatayev:] "They killed him almost before my eyes." [P. 1241]

[Pierre to Nikolai Rostov:] "Well, everything is going to ruin! Robbery in the law courts, in the army nothing but flogging, drilling, and Military Settlements . . ." [P. 1298]

Now, one may believe this was merely the literary artist gripping, as it were, his readers by the lapels to hold their attention, but before the Shabunin affair Tolstoy's sights were on other targets; after it he may have been compensating for an experience he would not speak of, as in a conversation he had with a remarkable young man who visited Yasnaya Polyana in 1868, the year after Stasyulevich's suicide. The visitor's name was Eugene Schuyler, and he was an American, the American consul in Moscow.

I call him a remarkable young man, and so he was. He was born in Ithaca, New York, on February 26, 1840, and was graduated from Yale, fifth in his class of 105, when he was nineteen. In 1861 he was one of the first three candidates ever to receive a Ph.D. from Yale (or any other university on the North American continent), and two years later he got a law degree from Columbia, so that he was twenty-three and practicing law in New York in 1863 when a small fleet of Russian warships sailed into New York Harbor, ostensibly on a goodwill mission of support for the North in the American Civil War, in fact to be out of the Baltic Sea, poised to attack British shipping, if England went to war with Russia to aid an uprising that was then going on in Poland.

The fleet's arrival enchanted New Yorkers. They turned out to entertain its officers, one of whom was a twenty-two-year-old cadet (soon to be promoted to the rank of midshipman) named Nikolai Rimsky-Korsakov, a budding composer. One of those who turned out was Eugene Schuyler.

Schuyler was so interested in the officers he met that he sought out an Orthodox priest and began to learn Russian, and so interested in the language that a Russian officer gave him a copy of Turgenev's *Fathers and Sons*. *Fathers and Sons* is a story of the conflict between generations—an older, more conservative generation and a younger, more challenging one typified by Bazarov, "a man who bows before no authority, however venerated it may be, and accepts no principle unproved." Schuyler liked it and got permission from Turgenev to translate it into English. When the translation appeared, in the early summer of 1867 (the first in English of a Turgenev novel), it attracted so much attention that Schuyler was promptly appointed American consul in Moscow. Giving up the law, he sailed for Europe in September. First stop: Baden Baden, the fashionable watering place in Germany where Turgenev was resting after finishing *Smoke*. There the two men, Schuyler at twenty-seven and Turgenev at forty-nine, got on so well together that Turgenev advised him to translate Tolstoy's novel *The Cossacks* (first published in 1863), which was, said the gentle Turgenev, "the finest and most perfect product of Russian literature." And when Schuyler left to continue his journey, he bore with him from Turgenev letters of introduction to leading Russian writers of the day, including Tolstoy, whom Turgenev had not seen or exchanged letters with since the two men had challenged each other to a duel in 1861 and 1862.

Schuyler arrived in Moscow and soon plunged into consular work, which delayed him somewhat as work sometimes does, but he met Tolstoy at a dinner one night and told him of Turgenev's suggestion. Tolstoy, whose work had not been translated into English, was pleased, and so he invited the young man to visit Yasnaya Polyana. When the night train pulled out of Moscow on September 21, 1868, Schuyler was aboard.

It was *rasputitsa*, the season of bad roads, and a cold, driving rain was sweeping the platform at Yasenki station when Schuyler got off at two o'clock in the morning. Tolstoy's coach was waiting for him, but the highway was so muddy and the night so dark that it took an hour and a half to reach Yasnaya Polyana, only three miles away.

The entrance towers to the estate! The avenue of birch and linden trees! The stables and courtyard, and beyond them Tolstoy's stone house, where everyone except a waiting servant was fast asleep. Schuyler went to bed but was up by eleven o'clock, when breakfast of coffee, bread, and butter was served as usual. There then began as wild a routine as Schuyler had ever experienced: hunting every day (he had never fired a gun before), dinner with the children at five o'clock, supper without the children at nine o'clock, talk until one or two o'clock in the morning.

Usually they went hunting with Tolstoy's friend Bibikov ("a pleasant, hospitable country gentleman with a good house and an agreeable family"), and usually they stood by the side of a country lane at the edge of a forest while Tolstoy's dogs drove in the hares. But one day a special affair was arranged, and they all rode out on horseback or by carriage to a great field and the top of a low hill, where the servants got things ready for lunch for Tolstoy, Schuyler, Bibikov and his two sons, Sonya, and whoever else happened to be around. Then Schuyler saw something he had never heard of before, nor have I in any other account of life with Tolstoy. While Sonya and Schuyler watched from the brow of the hill where the servants were spreading the blankets and laying out the food, Tolstoy, Bibikov, and Bibikov's sons mounted their horses and rode down into the field, "armed," says Schuyler, "with long, flexible, but heavy whips" and followed by dogs trained for the exercise. Once released, the dogs circled about, flushed hares from their feeding or hiding places, and chased them toward the hunters, who "deftly killed them with one blow of the whip, either strangling them or breaking their backs."

"It was," says Schuyler, "mad, break-neck riding over the hills, gullies, and blind holes, and the sport was almost as exciting to the onlookers as to the actual participants."

Back at the house, before and after dinner, there was much talk, with Tolstoy, who wore his gray, plaited blouse ("neither exactly a shooting jacket, nor yet a peasant shirt"), doing most of the talking. He spoke of his family and his farm, which had grown to some 3,000 acres but still was not a paying proposition; he was planting birch trees to be harvested for firewood in twenty years. His earliest known ancestor, he said, was a Dane named Dick, and the title had come down from Peter Tolstoy, a confidant of Peter the Great, who is best known perhaps for having tortured to death with royal approval the tsar's disobedient son Alexis.

But the time came when the subject turned to *The Cossacks*, which Tolstoy had sold unfinished to *The Russian Herald* to pay a gambling debt. Tolstoy agreed that Schuyler might translate it. (He did so, and the book came out ten years later.)

The time also came, as it often did at Yasnaya Polyana, when the talk turned to capital punishment, and Tolstoy then did what he often did for the rest of his life. He spoke not of the Shabunin affair (or so I presume, because Schuyler does not mention it), but of the death by guillotine he had witnessed in 1857. The one subject, it would seem, was taboo, the other fit for conversation.

He spoke of it "in such a vivid way," says Schuyler, "that I fully expected he would use it in a novel."[6]

He never did, neither Richeux's death by guillotine nor Shabunin's death by firing squad.

9

The Spiritual Crisis

One would think that by the 1870s Tolstoy's defenses against fears and doubts should have been impregnable. He was physically strong and creatively alert. He had a growing family and an expanding purse, and he was seldom idle. In 1870, 1871, and 1872 he worked on a novel about Peter the Great, read Pushkin, Gogol, Molière, Goethe, and Shakespeare, studied philosophy, learned Greek, and translated into Russian some of Xenophon, Herodotus, and Homer. He traveled to the Bashkir country beyond the Volga, reopened his school for peasant children at Yasnaya Polyana, and brought out an *ABC* book for teachers. From 1873 to 1877 he wrote *New ABC* and *Anna Karenina.* In 1878 and early 1879 he went back to a book he had begun before *War and Peace,* a story about the Decembrists, the army officers and their supporters who launched a liberal revolt against Nicholas I in 1825 and died, most of them, in prison, in Siberian exile at hard labor, or while serving long terms in the army as common soldiers. And yet along about the year 1874 something began to gnaw at Tolstoy's soul. It took the form of reflections on death and the meaning of life and drove him first to despair, then to God. He became a born-again Christian, but one of his own persuasion, who found no solace in organized religion and ultimately denied the divinity of Christ. Like those penitents who "come to Jesus" under the spell of zealous evangelists, he acknowledged and condemned the error of his ways; but unlike them, he found life's meaning in God without benefit of clergy, and the effect on him was profound. He stopped writing novels and embarked on a crusade that had as its theme the Sermon on the Mount.

One wonders what triggered the turning. Stefan Zweig looked for an answer and found none. He says Tolstoy "suddenly received a blow—a blow from somewhere out in the dark," that he suffered a shock that "has no name and really no visible cause."[1] Troyat says he was not happy:

> Or rather, the form of happiness that had become his lot did not content him and he wondered whether there might not be some other kind. His thoughts were haunted by the night at Arzamas [in 1869, when Death appeared before him in a terrifying dream]. Sometimes he did not read a single page or write a line for days on end. Along with mental paralysis came physical indifference. An automaton went through the motions of everyday life in his place. Then, suddenly, he awoke and began to ask questions, and apathy would give way to anguish.[2]

Simmons found an explanation in Tolstoy's propensity for self-examination and self-condemnation and in a search for God based on reason only. He points out, however: "What was about to take place in his spiritual life did not represent a change or a break with the past, but rather an intensification of a development that had been proceeding slowly ever since his youth."[3] R. F. Christian, who has translated 608 of Tolstoy's letters, appears to agree:

> The germ of almost everything that came to fruition in his thinking and writing after 1880 can be found in one or

other of his letters of the previous thirty years: his paci-
fism, his rejection of capital punishment, his hostility towards state institutions and bureaucratic practices, his un-
conventional views on primary and secondary education,
his distrust of university professors, doctors, and journalists, his hatred of big cities and an urban society based on
the buying and selling of property, his painful awareness
of the contrast between his own material well-being and
the poverty surrounding him, and his concern to justify his
art in terms of its usefulness to the community as a whole.
. . . It was almost certainly his constant obsession with the
phenomenon of mortality which impelled Tolstoy to seek a
religious solution to the purpose of existence which would
reconcile him to the bitter but inevitable fact that he too
must die."[4]

But why the "constant obsession"? Was it because fifteen
years after the fact he began to think of his beloved brother
Nikolai, who died literally in his arms in 1860? Or because
he could not get over the nightmare he had in Arzamas in
1869? Or because as he neared his fiftieth birthday in 1878
he came to realize that the grave—his grave—lay just beyond
the horizon?

It may have been all of these things and more, including, I
think, when he reflected on the case, feelings of guilt and
remorse over the death of a simple soldier in a field near
Yasnaya Polyana in the summer of 1866. On visits to relatives and friends and hunting trips to the south he often
passed by that field.

There are clues. The critical years were the years of *Anna
Karenina*, and *Anna Karenina* suggests the nature of his problem and the salvation toward which he was moving.[5]

[Levin:] "Who am I? What am I? A nobody, wanted by
no one and of no use to anyone." [P. 98]

The Enigmatic Years

Another voice inside [Levin] was saying that one must not submit to the past and one can make what one likes of oneself. [P. 107]

[Anna] felt herself clad in an impenetrable armor of falsehood. [P. 157]

That life [Kitty's spiritual life] was disclosed in religion, but a religion that had nothing in common with the religion Kitty had known since childhood and which found expression in morning and evening Mass . . . [P. 233]

[Levin] saw death and the approach of death in everything. [P. 360]

It was wrong, of course, but it was better not to think about such terrible details. [P. 467]

. . . but [Seryozha] knew his own mind, it was dear to him, and he guarded it as the eyelid guards the eye . . . [P. 528]

Anna goes to the railroad station and throws herself under an oncoming train:

And at that very instant she was horror-struck at what she was doing. "Where am I? What am I doing? Why?" She tried to get up, to throw herself back, but something huge and implacable struck her on the head and dragged her down on her back. "Lord, forgive me everything!" she cried, feeling the impossibility of struggling. The little peasant, muttering something, was working over the iron. And the candle, by the light of which she had been reading the book . . . flared up with a brighter light than before, lit up for her all that had hitherto been shrouded in darkness, flickered, began to grow dim, and went out forever. [P. 760]

The Spiritual Crisis

One thinks the novel has come to an end, that Tolstoy has said all he has to say, but there on the facing page is Part VIII, and Part VIII is a new, reborn Tolstoy speaking through the lips of Levin:

> Ever since Levin, at the sight of his beloved dying brother, looked for the first time at the questions of life and death in the light of what he called the new convictions . . . he had been horrified not so much by death as by life without the slightest knowledge of its origin, its purpose, its reason, and its nature. [P. 777]

> He, an unbeliever, began to pray, and while praying, he believed. [P. 778]

> To begin with, he was struck by the idea that the comprehension of divine truths is not given to man as an individual but to the totality of men united by love—the church. . . . But on reading afterward the history of the church by a Catholic writer and another by a Greek Orthodox writer and seeing that the two churches, both in their essence infallible, each repudiated the other, he became disappointed also in Khomyakov's doctrine of the church and that edifice, too, crumbled into dust as the philosophers' edifices had done. [P. 779]

> Realizing then for the first time that there was nothing for every man to look forward to except suffering, death, and everlasting oblivion, he had decided that to live like that was impossible, and that he had either to find an explanation of life so that it should not seem to be a wicked mockery of some devil or to shoot himself. . . . "Was it by reason that I attained to the knowledge that I must love my neighbor and not throttle him?" [P. 788]

> And it seemed to him now that there was not a single dogma of the church which could destroy the principal

99

thing—belief in God and in goodness as the only goal of man's existence. [P. 790]

In the drumfire of passionate repetition the reader feels the importance to Tolstoy of Part VIII, which Katkov refused to publish and Tolstoy put out independently in the late spring of 1877. Through Levin Tolstoy revealed his own awakening and some of its consequences: hatred of war (an old feeling but stronger now), love of God, contempt for such jingoist journalists as Katkov, who fanned the fires of patriotism. Before hitting on the formula, he was dissatisfied. "My God," he wrote to his friend Nikolai Strakhov, the literary critic, in late 1875, "if only someone would finish *A. Karenina* for me."[6] But as Russia moved toward war with Turkey early in 1877, all became clear. Levin speaks:

"Yes, well, my theory, you see, is that, on the one hand, war is such a bestial, cruel, and horrible thing that no man —let alone a Christian—can take upon himself personally the responsibility of starting a war." [P. 795]

He could not admit that a score of people, including his brother, had the right to assert, on the strength of what they were told by a few hundred volunteers with the gift of gab who came to Moscow, that together with the newspapers they were expressing the will and the thoughts of the people, especially when those thoughts found expression in vengeance and murder. [P. 800]

At the close Levin is still talking to himself:

"I shall still get angry with my coachman Ivan; I shall still argue and express my thoughts inopportunely; there will still be a wall between the holy of holies of my soul and other people, even my wife, and I shall still blame her for my own fears and shall regret it; I shall still be unable to understand with my reason why I am praying, and I shall continue to pray—but my life, my whole life, independently of anything that may happen to me, every moment of it, is no longer meaningless as it was before, but has an incontestable meaning of goodness, with which I have the power to invest it." [P. 807]

In the end the reader is unsure what brought on this soul-searching. Doubts, fears, questions about the meaning of life, to be sure. But why the doubts, why the fears, why the questions?

Tolstoy does not say, perhaps because for him, as for Levin, there was a wall between the holy of holies of his soul and other people, a wall he guarded "as the eyelid guards the eye," even in personal letters when he appeared to be most candid, even in *Confession*, which he wrote not long after *Anna Karenina*. *Confession* was Tolstoy speaking for Tolstoy and a confession in the sense that it was an acknowledgment of faith. As an explanation of his spiritual awakening, however, it reads like a statement intended more for effect than for revelation.

"I put men to death in war," he wrote, "I fought duels to slay others, I lost at cards, wasted my substance wrung from the sweat of peasants, punished the latter cruelly, rioted with loose women, and deceived men. Lying, robbery, adultery of all kinds, drunkenness, violence, murder . . . There was not one crime which I did not commit, and yet I was not the less considered by my equals a comparatively moral man" (p. 25).[7]

He "put men to death in war"? There is no evidence that he did. He "fought duels to slay others"? When? With whom? He committed murder? Not unless by murder he meant his military service in the Caucasus and Crimea. Determined to show what a terrible fellow he had been, he said he was "christened and educated in the Orthodox Christian faith" but by the time he was eighteen had "discarded all belief" in everything he had been taught. Lacking faith, he came to believe in what he called "the doctrine of general perfectability"—in "progress." Only at infrequent intervals were his feelings "roused against the common superstition of our age, which leads men to ignore their own ignorance of life." They were roused, he recalled, during his trip to France in 1857:

> Thus, during my stay in Paris, the sight of a public execution revealed to me the weakness of my superstitious belief in progress. When I saw the head divided from the body, and heard the sound with which they fell separately into the box, I understood, not with my reason, but with my whole being, that no theory of the wisdom of all established things, nor of progress, could justify such an act; and that if all the men in the world from the day of creation, by whatever theory, had found this thing necessary, I knew it was not necessary, it was a bad thing, and that therefore I must judge of what was right and necessary, not by what men said and did, not by progress, but what I felt to be true in my heart." [P. 28]

But not a word about Shabunin; not a word, as he wrote of death, about a terrible series of deaths in his own family from late 1873 to late 1875:

His son Petya died November 9, 1873, aged seventeen months.

Tatyana Yergolski, his father's second cousin, died June 20, 1874. Aunt Tatyana, who lived at Yasnaya Polyana, had brought Tolstoy up after the death of his mother.

His son Nikolai died February 20, 1875, aged ten months.

A daughter was born prematurely on October 30, 1875, and died the same day. (A week later, while Sonya was still in bed, the Tolstoys had house guests, among them her older brother Alexander, an officer in the Preobrazhensky Guards, and, perhaps surprisingly, Grigori Kolokoltsov.)

Aunt Pelageya Yushkov died December 22, 1875. Aunt Pelageya, Tolstoy's guardian after his father's death, lived at Yasnaya Polyana after Aunt Tatyana died.

These family tragedies, like Shabunin's execution, were, it would appear, matters that concerned "the holy of holies" of Tolstoy's soul, and *Confession* was for "other people."

> My life had come to a stop. I was able to breathe, to eat, to drink, to sleep, and I could not help breathing, eating, drinking, sleeping; but there was no real life in me because I had not a single desire, the fulfillment of which I could feel to be reasonable. [P. 31]

> I could not even wish to know the truth, because I guessed in what it consisted. The truth was, that life was meaningless. [P. 32]

> The horror of the darkness was too great to bear, and I longed to free myself from it as speedily as possible by a rope or a pistol ball. [P. 33]

> I sought it [an explanation of the questions that tormented him] in all branches of knowledge, and not only did I fail, but, moreover, I convinced myself that all those who had searched like myself had likewise found nothing; and not only had found nothing, but had come, as I had, to the despairing conviction, that the only absolute knowledge man can possess is this—that life is without meaning. [P. 34]

And so, Tolstoy says, he turned to the masses:

> Thus I began to study the lives and the doctrines of the people, and the more I studied the more I became con-

vinced that a true faith was among them, that their faith was for them a necessary thing, and alone gave them a meaning in life and a possibility of living. [P. 38]

During the whole of that year, when I was asking myself almost every minute whether I should or should not put an end to it all with a cord or a pistol, during the time my mind was occupied with the thoughts which I have described, my heart was oppressed by a tormenting feeling. This feeling I cannot describe otherwise than as a searching after God. [P. 41]

After this I began to retrace the process which had gone on within myself, the hundred times repeated discouragement and revival. I remembered that I had lived only when I believed in a God. As it was before, so it was now; I had only to know God, and I lived; I had only to forget Him, not to believe in Him, and I died. [P. 42]

Tolstoy tells but he does not explain. He continues:

What was this discouragement and revival? I do not live when I lose faith in the existence of a God; I should long ago have killed myself, if I had not had a dim hope of finding Him. I really live only when I am conscious of Him and seek Him. "What more then, do I seek?" A voice seemed to cry within me. "This is He, He without whom there is no life. To know God and to live are one. God is life."
Live to seek God, and life will not be without God. And stronger than ever rose up life within and around me, and the light that then shone never left me again. [P. 42]

It is all rather puzzling. One understands Tolstoy's conversion to God and his turning away from the church, but the *why* is unclear, perhaps because *Confession* is unclear. Tolstoy's biographers view it in various ways. Simmons sees it as "one of the noblest and most courageous utterances of man"—"executed with complete sincerity."[8] Troyat says it shows "a desire for total honesty" but adds: "He struts in his rags, he wallows in sham humility, and more than ever, reviling himself, he adores himself."[9] Dole writes: "It would almost seem as if there entered into *My Confession* [his title for the book] something of the fictional element."[10] And D. S. Mirsky calls it "a work of great imaginative sincerity."[11]

What was it, then? The truth? More or less. Nothing but the truth? More or less. But the whole truth? Few men acknowledge more.

10

In Moral Combat

Tolstoy's "spiritual awakening" in the 1870s—or his "conversion," as it has been called—might have been no more than that, an experience that concerned only himself and his God, if all he sought in that time of torment were answers to his questions about the meaning of life. But evidently something else troubled him, for no sooner had he seen the light of Christian ethics and morality than he began to spread it with fervor. He had spoken occasionally in *War and Peace*, insistently in *Anna Karenina*, and with still greater force in *Confession*. It was not enough. The Christian state put men to death, imprisoned them, exiled them, maintained armies of conscripts, and waged war; yet Jesus had taught forgiveness of one's enemies and love of one's neighbor. The Christian church assisted at executions and prayed for the success of Russian arms; yet Jesus had preached: "Ye have heard that it was said, An eye for an eye and a tooth for a tooth: But I say unto you, Resist not him that is evil. But whosoever smiteth thee on the right cheek, turn to him the other also." And in these contradictions or violations of expectation Tolstoy found the cause he was seeking. He would study Christ's teachings, proclaim them, explain them, and in the process challenge and call to account the tsar, his cabinet ministers, generals, priests, judges, police chiefs, jailers, revolutionary terrorists, the army, the Holy

Synod, the criminal code, the civil code, the military regulations—in short, everybody and everything, from patriotism
to the ownership of private property, that in his judgment
employed or excited or condoned or invited violence in any
form. It has been suggested that if he had been alive in 1917
there would have been three rival factions instead of two:
those who supported the tsarist regime, those who opposed
it, and Leo Tolstoy.

He had a problem, however. Jesus had said: "Resist not
him that is evil." Did this mean he was not to resist an evil
state and an evil church? Tolstoy went back to the early
Greek texts of the New Testament and convinced himself
that Christ meant one could resist evil provided one did not
resist by violent means. Once satisfied that this interpreta-
tion was correct, he set sail on a Christian course of his own.
In his opposition to the death penalty, it was no longer
sufficient to picture the horrors of the Paris guillotine, as he
had pictured them to Schuyler and in *Confession*; capital punishment was murder wherever it was imposed and for whatever reason. It was no longer possible to tolerate military
conscription or even voluntary service in the armed forces;
war was murder. He wrote in 1880 *An Examination of Dogmatic Theology*, an analysis of what he considered to be the
false dogmas of the church, and quickly followed it in 1881
with his *Union and Translation of the Four Gospels*, an interpre-
tation of their meaning. And when, after repeated attempts,
terrorists succeeded in assassinating Alexander II on March
1, 1881, he wrote a long letter to his son Alexander III beg-
ging him to pardon those who had killed his father, pleading with him to return good for evil, give them money, and
send them off to America.

"What are revolutionaries?" he asked rhetorically.

They are people who hate the existing order of things, find
it evil, and envisage the foundations of a future, better

order of things. One cannot fight them by killing and destroying them. It is not their number which is important but their ideas. To fight against them one must fight spiritually. . . . To fight against them, one must oppose their ideal with another ideal which will be superior to and will include their ideal. . . . There is only one ideal which can be opposed to them. It is the one from which they have themselves proceeded, without understanding it and blaspheming it, one which includes their ideal—the ideal of love, forgiveness, and the returning of good for evil.[1]

The terrorists were hanged, but Tolstoy pressed on in his role of articulate, nonviolent subversive who believed in the Sermon on the Mount, with which all Christians were familiar, some proclaiming it in earnest, others mouthing it as if it were not to be taken seriously. He most objected to state violence and the church's justification of it. Says Simmons:

His religion, then, amounted to a series of precepts that made life worth living, and which, if sincerely practiced, would enable him to accomplish the greatest amount of good. He had the courage to preach this religion and to give it force by sincerely attempting to live it. And he proclaimed his faith in the teeth of a powerful and jealous church that was scandalized by his exposure of its fraudulent dogmas, and in the face of a scornful science and materialistic philosophy that often ignored the existence of moral law.[2]

Courageous he was. It was more difficult then than now to swim against the current of conventional thought, for in striking out independently one risked not only the ridicule of friends and strangers but exile or solitary confinement in a monastery cell on orders of the Holy Synod. Tolstoy, however, did as he saw fit. In 1879 he threw out of his house a man who seriously proposed that convicts be blinded by their jailers to prevent their escape. In March of the same year he asked his cousin Alexandra to appeal to the tsar on behalf of three schismatic bishops ("one is 90 years old, the other two are around 60—a fourth died in prison")[3] who had been locked in the monastery at Suzdal for twenty-two years. In April he wrote sarcastically to his friend Fet about men "who shoot men for the good of humanity."[4] And writing to his friend Nikolai Strakhov at the end of the year, he summed up his thinking in words that were as rarely heard in his time as they are in ours: "Do God's works, carry out the will of the Father . . ."[5]

They were hard times. In May 1880 he passed up an opportunity to appear on the same platform with Dostoyevsky at the unveiling of the Pushkin monument in Moscow. In September he told Strakhov, Dostoyevsky's biographer, that he had just reread *Notes from the House of the Dead* and did not know "a better book in modern literature, Pushkin included."[6] Then in early 1881 Dostoyevsky died, and Tolstoy was floored at his passing. "How I should like to be able to say all I feel about Dostoyevsky," he wrote Strakhov.

I never saw the man and never had any direct relations with him, and suddenly when he died I realized that he was the very closest, dearest and most necessary man for me. I was a writer, and all writers are vain and envious—I at least was that sort of writer. But it never occurred to me to measure myself against him, never. Everything that he did (every good and real thing that he did) was such that the more he did it, the happier I was. Art arouses envy in me, and so does intelligence, but the things of the heart arouse only joy. I always considered him my friend, and I never thought otherwise than that we should meet, and that it was my fault that we hadn't managed to do so yet. And suddenly during dinner—I was late, and dining alone —I read that he was dead. Some support gave way under me. I was overcome; but then it became clear how precious he was to me, and I cried and am still crying. . . .[7]

The Enigmatic Years

As the months went by it became increasingly apparent that Tolstoy was no longer interested in writing novels. Sonya grew angry, Turgenev concerned. She gloried in assisting a genius whose work she admired and whose companionship she adored (when he was in a friendly mood), but as religious thinker and political gadfly he irritated her beyond measure. There was no money in it; it was a waste of talent, humiliating to her, harmful to the children, bad for him. So she fought him all the way, and he, as was his nature, fought back, not with explanation and persuasion, but with tight-lipped determination. When in 1881 the family moved to Moscow to be near their oldest sons, who were entering school, she threw herself into the aristocratic life of the town and, to Tolstoy's horror, hired uniformed servants to wait on table with white gloves. She attended concerts, went to the theater, made social calls, and entertained at home—on her children's behalf—while he, wearing his gray homemade blouse, prowled the slums of the city, overwhelmed by the chasm that separated the wealthy from the poverty-stricken, the healthy from the sick and the dying. He was not the man he had been and no longer wished to be. Disturbed by what he saw and heard, he directed the liveried servants to stop calling him "count" and address him as Leo Nikolayevich.

All plainly necessary to Tolstoy, but as word of his religious works—including *What I Believe*, which he wrote in early 1883—leaked out (all were banned by the censor but circulated privately), there came from distant France the now-famous penciled appeal from Turgenev: "Kind and dear Leo Nikolayevich," he wrote from Paris a few months before his death on August 22, 1883. (After a break that lasted seventeen years the two men had become reconciled on Tolstoy's initiative in 1878.)

It is long since I wrote you, for I have been and am, speaking frankly, on my deathbed. I cannot recover—there is no use thinking of it. I am writing to you particularly to tell you how glad I am to have been your contemporary, and to express to you my last, sincere request. My friend, return to literary activity! That gift came to you from whence comes all the rest. Ah, how happy I should be if I could think that my request would have an effect on you!! I am a doomed man—even the doctors do not know what to call my malady, *Névralgie stomacale goutteuse*. [He had cancer of the spine.] I can neither walk, nor eat, nor sleep. It is even wearisome to repeat all this! My friend, great writer of the Russian land, heed my request! Let me know if you receive this bit of paper, and permit me once more to embrace you *heartily*, heartily, and your wife and all yours. I can write no more, I am weary.[8]

The mind can scarcely conceive a more pathetic appeal, but to this unselfish moan from the deathbed Tolstoy did not reply. Perhaps he felt that what he wrote—what he felt he now had to write—was none of Turgenev's business, or that Turgenev's premise was invalid, that he needed no urging, that he would write again creatively when he could and not before. Indeed, immediately after *What I Believe*, while *What Then Must We Do* was in the works, he was already planning a return to short fiction when he received Turgenev's letter. *The Death of Ivan Ilyich* was in something like draft form, and he published it three years later along with two tales, *Nicholas Stick* and the exquisite *How Much Land Does a Man Need*, and a play based on a peasant crime, *The Power of Darkness*. *Nicholas Stick* is really a sermon built around an imaginary interview with an old soldier "on the threshold of death," who feels no remorse about the floggings and other punishments he witnessed or had a hand in ("The subalterns beat the young soldiers to death").

Meanwhile, the strain was becoming almost unbearable both for the born-again Christian, who by the early summer of 1884 was fifty-five years old, and his wife, who at thirty-nine had been pregnant much of her married life. Despite the deaths of three children, they now had nine: Sergei (born 1863), Tatyana (1864), Ilya (1866), Leo (1869), Marya (1871), Andrei (1877) Mikhail (1879), Alexei (1881), and Alexandra (1884), but there was little laughter heard around the house now.

In earlier days, when the children asked Tolstoy where he was born, he would point to the tops of the trees growing where the dismantled mansion had stood between its small stone wings and say: "Up there, where the top of that larch waves; that's where my mother's room was, where I was born on a leather sofa."[9]

Recalling those days, Ilya wrote many years later:

> In the summer we sometimes went over, the whole family together, to pay Uncle Seryozha [Tolstoy's only surviving brother, Sergei] a visit.
>
> It was a journey of twenty miles through open country to Pirogovo. On the road we passed Yasenki and [Novaya] Kolpna. It was somewhere there, my mother told us, that papa defended a soldier before a Court-martial for insulting an officer. He was condemned and taken out at once and shot in the fields. It was horrible to think of. Perhaps it was in accordance with the law, but to us children it was incomprehensible."[10]

"Mother" told us—not "papa." One may infer that papa did not wish to discuss it or that he had other matters on his mind or both. He clearly had much to think of in the summer of 1884, for a transformation was taking place within him. He was changing from a born-again Christian to a born-again Christian with decidedly puritanical views. It seemed to him now that one who loved God should not smoke, drink, or kill any of God's creatures, so after a considerable struggle he gave up smoking, drinking, and hunting, his favorite sport; and because it seemed to him that if one should not kill for meat one should not eat meat, he became a vegetarian. Along about the same time he took to shoe-making and helping the peasants with mowing and the har-vest in the belief that there was something divine about physical labor and the sweat of the brow. This behavior, too, Sonya might have tolerated had it not been for his continu-ing refusal to return to long fiction and his increasing insis-tence that the educational system and social customs of the day were bad for the children. That attitude almost drove her out of her mind. A rich man now, he did not want them to grow up like the sons and daughters of a rich man, but to work with their hands, love God and their neighbors, think about the welfare of others and not of their own material comfort. The older ones obliged him up to a point. They joined him in the fields, though his religious views and new convictions left most of them unmoved.

It was different outside of the family circle. Many Rus-sians, some miserably poor, others wealthy, were attracted by his message of nonviolence. Disciples began to come aboard, among them in 1884 a giant of a man, Vladimir Chertkov, thirty years old and a former officer in the Horse Guards, and Pavel Biryukov, twenty-four and a recent grad-uate of the Naval Academy, whom Chertkov introduced to Tolstoy. With the help of these two men, who stayed with him (when not in exile on his account or doing his work abroad) for the remaining years of his life (Chertkov became the executor of his will, Biryukov his biographer), a publish-ing house, the Intermediary, was established to print cheap booklets of good literature for the masses. The Intermediary was so successful that in the first four years of its existence it sold 12 million copies at one and a half kopecks apiece (three-quarters of a cent).

Tolstoy was seldom busier than during this period. Driven by his beliefs to dogmatic works and by a creative urge to fiction of one kind or another, he pressed other writers, such as Nikolai Leskov, Mikhail Saltykov-Shchedrin, and

Alexander Ostrovsky, to contribute to the Intermediary, and carried on at the same time a heavy correspondence. One has to believe he almost forgot—perhaps did forget temporarily—about the Shabunin affair and whatever influence it had on his great novels and spiritual awakening.

Not indefinitely, however, for suddenly in the spring of 1889 a man unknown to Tolstoy came into his life while he was working on *The Kreutzer Sonata* at a home he had bought in Moscow. A package was delivered to his door. Opening it, he found a manuscript and letter dated April 3 from one Nikolai Ovsiannikov. He had been, Ovsiannikov wrote, a junker, a cadet, in the Sixty-fifth Regiment when it was stationed near Yasnaya Polyana twenty-three years before. He had witnessed the execution and the demonstration of the peasants at the grave site, and it had occurred to him to tell the story, now that Tolstoy was a famous man. Accordingly, he had written the enclosed manuscript, titled "An Episode from the Life of Count L. N. Tolstoy." Would Tolstoy look it over? He wanted to be sure there were no errors of fact. He wanted more than that. He wanted Tolstoy to contribute additional details and give his permission for its publication.

It was a voice from the past—an unexpected, unwelcome voice that stirred painful memories. Nevertheless, Tolstoy read the manuscript, as he recorded in his diary on April 9, 1889: "Read the episode about the [or *an*, because there is no definite or indefinite article in Russian] executed soldier. Badly written, but the episode was terrible in the simplicity of the description—contrast between the corrupted colonel and officers ordering the eyes blindfolded and the peasant men and women having requiem mass officiated for the dead and collecting burial coins."[11]

Shabunin's name was not mentioned, and there was no suggestion in the entry that Tolstoy had anything to do with the affair. No one reading the diary (except Sonya and perhaps a few intimate friends such as Chertkov) would know what he was talking about.

Four days later Ovsiannikov called at the house to hear Tolstoy's decision in the matter. This time he merited a still more cryptic entry: "Later Ovsiannik[ov], about the article (on the defense of the [or *a*] soldier). 'Your Excellency.' What's to be done?"[12]

The words conceal Tolstoy's refusal that day to help Ovsiannikov. They reveal no more than that the two men met, the subject of their discussion, and Tolstoy's irritation at having been called "Your Excellency" seven years after he had dropped the use of his title. What was to be done to stop people from addressing him like that?

One senses tension in the air, the icy hostility with which Tolstoy received his visitor.

Undeterred, Ovsiannikov came back on the fifteenth and left a second letter, in which he urged Tolstoy to reconsider. Tolstoy replied the next day politely, firmly, and negatively in a four-sentence letter: "I am very sorry I cannot satisfy your wish; as I told you, all my life I have handled everything with respect to writings about me—translations, excerpts, and so forth—in the same manner: forbidding nothing and authorizing nothing. I cannot treat your article in any other way. Please do not be angry with me because of this. Really I cannot do otherwise."[13]

It was a weak excuse, and hardly true, for Tolstoy had helped other writers on other occasions in other circumstances. But the Shabunin affair was a matter he wanted nothing to do with, as one may gather from the fact that the two diary entries and the letter quoted here are the only surviving documents in which Tolstoy referred to the case in writing in the long forty-two years from 1866 to 1908. One may suspect there were other entries, other letters, later destroyed, but the suspicion serves no useful purpose, for

Tolstoy's way of dealing with the affair was not to meet it head on, not to wrestle it to the ground, but to compensate for it in his work.

Indeed, he almost gave away the game in *Resurrection*, which he had in the recesses of his mind when Ovsiannikov called on him in the spring of 1889, and which he began to write the following December.

11

Resurrection

"Every creative writer's work," says W. Somerset Maugham in an essay on Tolstoy,

> is, to some extent at least, a sublimation of instincts, desires, day-dreams, call them what you like, which for one cause or another he has repressed, and by giving them literary expression he is freed of the compulsion to give them the further release of action. But it is not a complete satisfaction. He is left with a feeling of inadequacy. That is the ground of the man of letters' glorification of the man of action and the unwilling, envious admiration with which he regards him. It may well be that Tolstoy engaged in manual labor in substitution for his rejected impulses. It is possible that he would have found in himself the strength to do what he sincerely thought right if he had not by writing his books taken the edge off his determination.[1]

It is possible, perhaps probable, but what makes Leo Tolstoy so difficult to come to grips with is that he was both a man of letters and a man of action. His vaulted room on the ground floor at Yasnaya Polyana was no ivory tower. It became his practice to visit the Tula jail, to sympathize with and comfort the prisoners, and on one occasion he entered a court case at Krapivna on behalf of the defendants, as Sonya recorded in her diary: "There was a trial on, and thanks to Lyova's intervention, the murderers got off with a very light sentence. Instead of penal servitude, they were only condemned to deportation."[2] Moreover, even in his role of man of letters he was a man of action, as he demonstrated most vividly in *Resurrection*, which he wrote off and on throughout the 1890s. In *Resurrection* he did more than take up the pen; he buckled on his armor, mounted his steed, seized his lance, and led the charge. And yet in this, his first full-length novel since *Anna Karenina*, there are traces of repressed instincts; there is certainly "glorification of the man of action" by the man of letters. One is struck by certain similarities and differences between *Resurrection* and the Shabunin affair.

You recall how the story opens. While serving on a jury that is trying a case of robbery and murder, Nekhludov recognizes one of the accused, Katusha (Katerina) Maslova, as the young girl he seduced years before. In the interim he has forgotten her. He knew "he had forfeited his self-respect and had lost all right to be considered the upright, noble-hearted, generous fellow he always meant to be. He could neither look an honest man in the eye nor blame a fellow sinner. And yet he had to keep up his self-respect if he wished to lead a pleasant life. There was only one way to do that: to forget the past" (p. 68).[3] He has forgotten but now remembers and wants to tell the court of his involvement. Yet "the dread of the disgrace which would befall him if all these people knew what he had done was stifling the remorse that struggled in his soul; for, at this stage of the affair, his strongest feeling was fear for himself" (p. 78). Nekhludov remains silent, but when Katusha is condemned to four years' penal servitude, because the presiding judge made a mistake in his charge to the jury, Nekhludov seeks him out, explains the error, talks to the prosecutor, and when he fails to have the sentence set aside, hires a lawyer, Fanarin.

One wonders. What if Tolstoy, the man of letters, had approached Colonel Yunosha after Shabunin's trial and conviction? So far as is known, he never did. What if later on he had tried to persuade him to delay the execution until the tsar acted on his appeal for clemency? So far as is known, he never did. What if he had hired a lawyer to help him press his petition? He never did. Given the revelations of the Moscow file, it is unlikely that any action by Tolstoy could have saved Shabunin, but he was unaware of its contents and had to live with the case as he understood it.

Walking home that first night, Nekhludov says to himself: "I am ashamed and disgusted, disgusted and ashamed." He is "horrified at the chasm that separated the life he was leading from the demands of his own conscience. . . . But the spiritual nature, which alone is true, alone powerful, alone eternal, had already awakened in Nekhludov, and he could not but trust it. However vast the disparity between what he was and what he wished to be, nothing could discourage this newly awakened spiritual being" (pp. 101–4). It sounds like Tolstoy's *Confession*, with this difference: that Nekhludov's conversion occurred overnight. "He prayed, asking God to enter into him and purify him; and while he was thus praying, it came to pass. God was dwelling in his awakened conscience. He found himself one with God—and, therefore, not only the freedom, the courage, and the joy of life became his own, but all the power of righteousness. The best a man could do, he now felt himself capable of doing" (p. 105).

As Tolstoy develops his story, the Shabunin affair comes repeatedly to mind: Katusha is a *meshchanka*, the feminine form of *meshchanin*, Shabunin's social status. She drinks heavily, as he did. There are three judges, as at his court-martial. One of them is "gloomy," as Stasyulevich was. The failure of the president of the court to tell the jury it can find Katusha guilty but "without intent to kill" (and thus release her from further imprisonment and punishment) recalls Tolstoy's failure to include the number of Shabunin's regiment in his petition to the tsar. Nekhludov tries to have the conviction set aside, as Tolstoy tried. He sees Katusha in prison, as Tolstoy saw Shabunin in the *izba* at Ozerki.

And now comes what Maugham calls the "glorification" of the man of action by the man of letters: Nekhludov goes to St. Petersburg to appeal the decision of the lower court. (Tolstoy stayed at Yasnaya Polyana.) Nekhludov sees his influential aunt. (Tolstoy only wrote to Alexandra.) Nekhludov takes his case to the Senate's court of appeals, a course that was not open to Tolstoy, but when the senators reject it on a split vote, the man of action presses on. Nothing deters him. He sees Selenin, the prosecutor who opposed reversal of the verdict, and again pleads Katusha's cause. (In the historical record there is no suggestion that Tolstoy sought out the man from Moscow who prosecuted Shabunin.)

Nekludov confers with his lawyer, who recommends a petition to the tsar, saying he will draft it for him. (Tolstoy had no help in drawing up his flawed appeal.)

Meanwhile, Nekhludov has returned to his diary after a lapse of two years. In it he tells all about the Maslova affair. (Tolstoy, who is believed to have kept no diary from 1865 to 1878, preserved no personal record of the Shabunin affair, unless the entries were later destroyed.)

Nekhludov follows Katusha to Siberia and there picks up his mail, which includes a recent copy of *The European Herald* (the journal that in real life was edited by Stasyulevich's older brother Mikhail) and "a registered letter in a strong envelope with a bright red seal." The man of action has won the day. Perseverance has paid off. The letter is from Selenin: "You were right about Maslova. I went over the case carefully and saw what a shocking injustice had been done to her. . . . I succeeded in helping the matter along and am now sending you a copy of the mitigation of sentence. . . ."

The mitigation of sentence, something like what Tolstoy

hoped and failed to receive in 1866, read as follows: "His Majesty's Office for the Reception of Petitions. Case No. —. Dept. —. Date —. By Order of the Chief of His Majesty's Office for the Reception of Petitions one *meshchanka* Katerina Maslova is hereby informed that in consequence of her petition His Majesty graciously condescends to grant her request and hereby orders that her sentence to hard labor be commuted to exile to some less remote place of Siberia."

Tolstoy finished his novel on December 18, 1899, ten years after he first sketched it in outline, and wrote in his diary that day: "Completed *Resurrection*. Not good, uncorrected, hurried, but it is done with and I am no longer interested."[4] Uncorrected it was in some minor details. Hurried it was in the ending. But it was judged better than good, had a better sale in the Western world than either *War and Peace* or *Anna Karenina* up to that time, and helped to make his reputation in England and America, where until then his works were not widely known. One notes that in the entry headed "Russian Literature" in the ninth edition of the *Encyclopaedia Britannica*, Turgenev merited an entire paragraph, Dostoyevsky a sentence and a half, and Tolstoy one sentence only: "Count L. Tolstoy is the author of a work of fiction describing the war of 1812 which has gained celebrity in Russia, *Voina i Mir (War and Peace)*." And this was as late as 1897.

Outwardly Tolstoy changed considerably during the writing of *Resurrection*. The artist Ilya Repin, a friend of Tolstoy's, has reported what he looked like in 1897: "Prominent cheek-bones, a rough-hewn nose, a long shaggy beard, enormous ears, a bold and determined mouth, brows jutting out over his eyes like plates of armor, a fierce, imposing, belligerent appearance"—much, one thinks, as he long had looked.[5] But he was thinner now. The chestnut hair and beard had turned first to gray, then to white. He still complained of pains in the stomach, and there were periods of illness when he thought he would die and sometimes hoped he would. Nevertheless, he was unusually strong. When he reached his seventieth birthday, in 1898, he could cut hay for two or three hours without resting, haul water from the well, go for walks that tired his younger companions, ride a bicycle, swim, ride horseback for twenty miles; and in manner he was as tough as he had ever been. In his battle with church and state he was relentless. In dealings with his older sons he was coldly disapproving and uncompromisingly stern, and in his relations with Sonya he insisted on working and living in his own way, conceding a little here and a little there only when he feared for her life or she nagged him to distraction. Every day, it seems, there was a struggle of one kind or another.

Toward the end of 1890 Sonya began to copy his diaries without his permission, evidently to draw upon them for one of her own (to be written later on) which would show posterity how much she was wronged by this man she adored, who in her view treated her so shabbily. (Her sister writes in her memoirs: "Sonya says in her diary which she began to keep in 1900, recollecting the past . . ."[6] Her daughter Alexandra writes in hers: "She [her sister Marya] was worried and agitated and told me that mother was writing a post-dated diary, using father's diary and interpreting the events and moods there to suit herself.")[7] Discovering what she was up to, Tolstoy hid his diary away, but soon another cause of dissension arose. Deeply concerned about the disparity between the life he led and the life he wished to lead, now believing it was wrong for him to make money from his works, he renounced in 1891 the copyrights to everything he had written after 1881 and everything he would write in the future. Sonya objected violently, although he had signed over to her the rights to everything he had written through 1881, including *War and Peace* and *Anna Karenina*, and, exceptionally, as a birthday present to her, *The Death of Ivan Ilyich*, which came out in 1886. Sonya screamed in opposition. He was making her a pauper, taking the food out of the mouths of her babies. She turned with increasing anger on his followers, those who found life's meaning in his dogmatic works and whom she referred to as "the dark ones." Her primary target was Chertkov, Tolstoy's leading disciple, who ran the Intermediary publishing house with Biryukov's help; and although she preferred Biryukov to Chertkov, she opposed Biryukov's courtship of her daughter Marya (Masha) and succeeded in breaking it off.

Tolstoy survived this quarrel, but partly to soothe Sonya's feelings and partly to do what he thought he ought to do, he renounced his property rights in 1892, dividing everything he owned (estimated to be worth 580,000 rubles, or about $290,000) into ten equal parts, one for Sonya and one for each of the nine children: Sergei, Tatyana, Ilya, Leo, Marya, Andrei, Mikhail, Alexandra, and Ivan, who was born in 1888, two years after the early death of Alexei.

Meanwhile, when he was not working away from home on famine relief, Tolstoy wrote on in the vaulted room of his Yasnaya Polyana house, which by this time had been tripled in size to accommodate his large family and the tutors and governesses who looked after the younger children. Occasionally sad news arrived. His friend Dyakov died in 1891, Fet in 1892. Occasionally, too, he turned to *Resurrection* or *Father Sergei*, but in this period he concentrated his attention on *The Kingdom of God Is within You*, an eloquent denunciation of war but a more powerful condemnation of governments, which in his opinion arm themselves and wage war because they are violent institutions and cannot do otherwise. He had no faith in disarmament conferences. Governments, he said, existed to rule the many on behalf of the few; they derived their power from the army; therefore, they would never disarm.

The tsar, the palace, the government, the aristocracy of St. Petersburg were aghast. How to deal with a man like that?

The Enigmatic Years

A man to whom nothing, so they thought, was sacred? It was not that he was on the side of revolutionary terrorists, for he condemned them as strongly as he did the security forces of the state. Asked what he considered to be the difference between a killing by a policeman and a killing by a terrorist, he said the same difference as between cat shit and dog shit, and he didn't like the smell of either one.

State and church were not amused. The police had harassed him before; now they tracked his every movement. Priests had denounced him before; now they spied on him. Friends feared, and enemies hoped, that he would be exiled or confined in a monastery, but Alexander III had no intention of making him a martyr. Instead, he hounded his followers and anyone with religious convictions that differed from those of the church, anyone who refused military conscription, anyone who was caught distributing or in possession of Tolstoy's censored works. No doubt feelings of satisfaction raced through aristocratic circles when he suffered defeat; he often did. No doubt, too, he hoped for better days in 1894, when Alexander III died and was succeeded by his son Nicholas II—"that unfortunate young man," Tolstoy called him later on. Unfortunate indeed, for Nicholas, his wife, Alexandra, and all five of his children were murdered in the cellar of a house in Ekaterinburg (Sverdlovsk) after the revolution of 1917.

Nicholas, however, soon let it be known he would follow in the footsteps of his father. When the young tsar (he was only twenty-six at the time) was urged by representatives of elective district councils (zemstvos) to institute liberal reforms, he replied that any such thoughts were "foolish daydreams." He would uphold the autocracy, he said, and proceeded to do so with the police and summary courts.

The year was 1895 and a turbulent one for Leo Tolstoy. It began with his completion in January of *Master and Man*, a beautifully told story of man's humanity to man in which a landowner sacrifices his life in a snowstorm for that of his servant. Like most of his recent fiction—like *Resurrection*, with which he was having trouble—it was a tale that combined the author's creative and dogmatic instincts, and it got him into the kind of difficulty he was eager to avoid, apparently without knowing how. He might have guessed that by promising *Master and Man* to the *Northern Herald* he would anger Sonya, who wanted it for his collected works, which she managed and which were the family's principal source of income. He might have known she would scream and yell and throw herself on the ground, and perhaps he did, thinking she would get over it. But he did not expect she would run from their Moscow home in bathrobe and slippers in the dead of winter, threaten suicide, seek death by exposure. Once before, to get what she wanted, she had threatened to throw herself under a train (like Anna Karenina). This time, as before, Tolstoy ran after her, dragged her back to the house, and gave in. He compromised. She could have *Master and Man* at the same time as the *Northern Herald* and the Intermediary, which now was being run by Biryukov.

No winner, no loser. Just agonizing turmoil quickly followed by tragedy. Little Ivan (Vanichka) fell ill and died of scarlet fever a few weeks before his seventh birthday. The fifth of the thirteen children to die, he was a friendly, kindly, interesting child, and the loss was almost more than the mother could bear. Leo withstood the shock by repeating to himself and telling others it was God's will, but he could not work. Days went by—one week, two weeks, three weeks— and he would come out of his room about noon without having written a line. For a while, then, Tolstoy and Sonya were drawn together, but soon the writer's urge and the polemicist's drive returned. He had something to say and had to say it, and so he went back to *Resurrection* in late winter. By summer he had a draft which, though it did not

The Enigmatic Years

satisfy him, he allowed Anton Chekhov to read when the young writer stopped by Yasnaya Polyana on the eighth and ninth of August.

About six weeks before, however, an incident occurred that significantly affected Tolstoy's life. The Dukhobors, a dissident religious sect that had been persecuted and exiled under Alexander I, Nicholas I, Alexander II, and Alexander III, burned their weapons on the night of June 28 to demonstrate their objection to military conscription and war. Young Nicholas II cracked down. Cossacks rode in and beat them, arrested their leaders, and exiled about 4,000 of them to distant mountain villages in the Caucasus, where they soon faced death by disease and starvation. Horrified by this atrocity, Tolstoy sent Biryukov to investigate and upon his return mailed Biryukov's report to *The Times* of London, together with an appeal of his own "to the court of world opinion." By this time he was in a state of nonviolent war with Nicholas, as he had been with his father, and he expressed his feelings and recommendations in a letter to an associate the following year:

> You [meaning the state] want to institute Land Captains with birch-rods instead of Justices of the Peace; that is your business, but we will not be tried by your Land Captains, nor will we ourselves be appointed to this office. You want to make trial by jury a mere formality; that is your business, but we will not serve as judges, or as lawyers, or as jurymen. You want to establish lawlessness under the cover of the "state of emergency"; that is your business, but we will not participate in it and will plainly call the "state of emergency" an illegality, and the death sentences inflicted without trial—murder. You want to set up classical grammar schools with military exercises and religious instruction, or Cadet Corps; that is your business, but we will not be teachers in them, or send our children to them, but will educate them as we consider best. You want to

reduce the zemstvo to a nullity; we will not participate in it. You forbid the printing of what you don't like; you can seize and burn books, and punish the printers, but you can't prevent us from writing and talking, and we shall do so. You order us to swear allegiance to the tsar; we will not do so, because it is stupid, false and base. You order us to serve in the army; we will not do so, because we consider mass murder to be an act just as offensive to our conscience as a single murder and, above all, the promise to kill whomever the commander orders is the basest act a man can perform. You profess a religion a thousand years behind the times, with the Iverskaya icon, relics and coronations; that is your business, but we not only do not acknowledge this idolatry and superstition to be religion, but we call it superstition and idolatry and are trying to rescue people from it.[8]

Such was Tolstoy's attitude in 1896, which was as trying a year for him as 1895. To his sorrow, his son Andrei joined the army, as his son Ilya had done in the 1880s and as Mikhail would do not long after. His friend Strakhov died. Sonya became infatuated with the composer Sergei Taneyev, and in November *The Russian Review* came out with Ovsiannikov's recollection of the Shabunin affair.

Did he read it again? He certainly received a copy, because Biryukov found one among his papers in 1908; if he read it, he may have had it in mind when in December he wrote an article titled *Help* and attached it to an appeal on behalf of the Dukhobors written by Chertkov, Biryukov, and I. M. Tregubov, another disciple. In it he advised his readers not to shrug off the appeal, but to recognize its importance:

As in the life of each separate individual (I know this in my own life, and everyone will find similar cases in his own), so also in the life of nations and humanity, events occur which constitute turning-points in their whole exis-

127

tence; and these events, like the "still small voice" . . . in which Elijah heard God, are always not loud, not striking, hardly remarkable; and in one's personal life one afterward regrets that at the time one did not guess the importance of what was taking place.

"If I had known it was such an important moment in my life," one always afterward thinks, "I should not have acted in such a way."[9]

When he penned these lines, was he thinking that if he had understood early enough the significance of the Shabunin case, he would have acted differently? Who knows? He could have been reflecting upon hundreds of things he did as a young man and of which he was ashamed. In any event, in *Help* he fought effectively for a humane cause, and the government evidently thought so too, for it struck back where it thought it would hurt. Alarmed by exaggerated reports of impending revolution, egged on by the Holy Synod, which believed that such religious dissidents as the Dukhobors were undermining the foundations of the Orthodox church, Nicholas II arrested and exiled Chertkov, Biryukov, and Tregubov—Chertkov to England, Biryukov and Tregubov to the Baltic provinces, from which they later were allowed to go to England.

Tolstoy was stunned but quickly recovered. Accompanied by Sonya—who, though herself an Orthodox believer, stood by Tolstoy on this occasion as she had often done in the past—he traveled to St. Petersburg in February 1897 to say goodbye to his friends and, not incidentally, to make the best of a distressing situation. As a consequence, although he would not see them again for seven years—not until after the tsar decreed an amnesty on the birth of his son and heir in 1904—their exile turned out to be more damaging to the state than to Tolstoy. Chertkov set up headquarters in England and from that vantage point printed and circulated

Tolstoyan propaganda. He made contact with non-Russians who thought as Tolstoy did about military conscription and war, and the first beneficiaries were the Dukhobors. Nicholas backed down. Overwhelmed by pressure from abroad and prodded by his remarkable mother, the dowager empress Marya Feodorovna, the former princess Dagmar of Denmark, he gave permission for about 10,000 Dukhobors to emigrate on the condition that some country would receive them and they would agree never to return. From that day in February 1898 events moved fairly quickly. Tolstoyans, Quakers, and like-minded men and women persuaded the Canadian government to accept them as settlers in the Far West. A campaign was organized to pay for their passage.

On April 1 Tolstoy wrote a letter to the *Daily Chronicle* in London, appealing for funds. Other letters to other newspapers in England and the United States followed.[10] That summer he told Chertkov he would contribute to the Dukhobor fund everything he would receive from the Russian and foreign rights to *Resurrection, Father Sergei,* and a story he was writing that eventually became known as *The Devil.*[11] On December 21, accompanied by Tolstoy's oldest son, Sergei, some 2,000 Dukhobors sailed from the Black Sea port of Batum for the New World. About 4,000 had left on other ships a few days before. The rest would follow.

And now, having sold the Russian serial rights to *Resurrection* for 12,000 rubles (about $6,000), he had to finish it; and finish it he did, in the face of one of the most difficult challenges a novelist can impose upon himself: to tell a story successfully and at the same time to express most dogmatically one's strongest opinions. In *Resurrection* Tolstoy fired simultaneously at church and state, and although he felt the kick of his verbal weapon in the reaction of the censors, he winged both targets.

Never before in novel form had he exposed the church to

such scorn and ridicule as he did during his description of the scene in the prison chapel before the convicts, including Katusha, set off for Siberia. Never before had he exposed in a novel the injustice of the state's judicial system. The chapel service, he wrote, was "a sacrilegious mockery of that same Christ in whose name it was being done."

> The essence of the service lay in the assumption that the small pieces of bread cut by the priest and dipped in the wine to the accompaniment of certain manipulations and prayers, became the body and blood of God. These manipulations consisted in the priest's raising his arms at stated intervals and, encumbered as he was with his cloth-of-gold robe, keeping them in this position, kneeling from time to time and kissing the table and all objects upon it. But the principal act came when the priest, having taken a napkin in both hands, slowly and rhythmically waved it over the saucer and the golden cup. This was supposed to be the moment when the bread and wine were transformed into flesh and blood, and therefore this part of the service was performed with special solemnity. [Pp. 134–35]

Tolstoy described the sacrament of the Eucharist and continued:

> The most important part of the Christian service was now over, but another service was added for the consolation of the prisoners. The priest stood in front of an image (with black hands and a black face, lit by a dozen wax candles, and covered with beaten gold) which was meant to represent the same God he had been eating, and in a strained falsetto voice, half singing, half speaking, he recited the following words: "Jesu, most sweet, glorified by the Apostles; Jesu, lauded by the martyrs, Almighty Lord, save me, Jesu my Saviour; Jesu most beautiful, have mercy on him who cries to Thee through the prayers of the Holy Virgin and of all Thy saints and Thy prophets; Jesu my Saviour,

make me worthy of the sweetness of Heaven, Jesu, Lover of me."

Then he paused, took breath, crossed himself, and bowed to the ground. All did likewise: the inspector, the warders, and the prisoners in the gallery with their clanking chains.

Tolstoy was not finished with a church that extended the cross to bound men who were about to be hanged or killed by firing squad. At the prison Nekhludov catches sight of a large painting of the Crucifixion hanging in a vaulted hall with small barred windows. "'Why should that be here?' he thought, his mind connecting the image of Christ with liberation and not with captivity" (p. 141).

Later on, he hears that two prisoners have been flogged. But corporal punishment has been abolished, he protests. "Not for those who have been deprived of civil rights," he is told (p. 178).

Hearing these words, Nekhludov is overwhelmed by moral nausea that is on the verge of becoming actual physical sickness. He looks around and sees in a corner of the room "a large image of Christ—as is usual in places where people are tortured" (pp. 178–79).

Early in his story Tolstoy goes for the throat of the judicial system and never lets go. At Katusha's trial with Nekhludov in the jury box:

After the last words of the prisoners, there was an argument lasting for some time about the form of the questions to be placed before the jury. This settled, the president began to sum up. Before stating the facts to the jury, he explained to them in a pleasant, informal tone of voice that burglary was burglary and theft was theft, that theft from a room that was locked was theft from a room that was locked, and that theft from an open room was theft from an open room. While offering these explanations, he looked repeatedly at Nekhludov, as though endeavoring to impress him with the importance of the information and in the hope that, understanding it, he would explain everything to the rest of the jury. Then he proceeded to elucidate another truth, namely that murder is a deed which aims at the death of a fellow creature, and that therefore poisoning is murder. When this truth also had, in his opinion, been sufficiently apprehended by the jury, he explained that if the crimes of theft and murder were committed simultaneously, this combination of crimes would be theft and murder. [Pp. 78–79]

When Katusha is convicted and sentenced because the presiding judge made a mistake in his charge to the jury, Nekhludov concludes that every law court is "not only a useless but an immoral institution"—that crime is punishment and punishment is a crime (p. 125). His lawyer, Fanarin, does nothing to disabuse him of the thought. Fanarin says: "We are in the habit of thinking that our prosecutors and judges are men of liberal views. Once upon a time that was so, but it is quite different in these days. They are simply officials whose chief interest is the twentieth day of the month, when their salaries become due—and which they'd like to see increased—and there their principles stop. They are prepared to accuse, try, and sentence anyone you like" (pp. 234–35).

In time, Nekhludov comes to believe with Henry David Thoreau, American poet, naturalist, and essayist who championed the individual against social organization and materialist civilization, that "under a government which imprisons anyone unjustly, the true place for a just man is also in prison" (p. 296).

Resurrection is about guilt, remorse, injustice, and a man's spiritual awakening; it has nothing to do with the army or military law. But Tolstoy did not let pass this opportunity to swoop on his familiar prey. In an effort to help a con-

vict other than Katusha as he works through high government contacts to assist her and the "sectarians" (religious
dissidents like the Dukhobors), Nekhludov calls on Baron
Kriegsmuth, an "old general" who is in charge of the horrifying prison fortress of Peter and Paul:

> He had seen many years of active service, but people said
> he was now in his dotage. The white cross, which he val-
> ued so highly, he had received in the Caucasus for com-
> manding close-cropped Russian peasants, dressed in uni-
> forms and armed with guns and bayonets, who had killed
> more than a thousand men bent on defending their homes
> and families. Afterward he had served in Poland, where
> he also compelled Russian peasants to commit all sorts of
> crimes, and for this he received more orders and decora-
> tions. [P. 260]

Tolstoy's anger and outrage did not slip into *Resurrection*.
Like a modern Martin Luther, he nailed it to the door for
all to see, feel, understand; but as Maugham suggests, this
sublimation of instincts, if that is what it was, was not a
complete satisfaction. He was left with "a feeling of inade-
quacy."

As he wrote in his diary: "Completed *Resurrection*. Not
good, uncorrected, hurried, but it is done with and I am no
longer interested."

12

The Church Strikes Back

Despite indications to the contrary, Leo Tolstoy did not live in a fishbowl. Like most famous men who keep diaries and copies of the letters they write, he intended to have them published and saw to it they would be. Accordingly, he made sure they reflected the image of himself he wished to project and on at least one occasion went so far as to censor what he had written. It was the summer of 1910, not long before his death, and he turned for help to Chertkov. A surviving letter from Chertkov to Tolstoy reads: "In view of your wish to resume possession of the diaries which you gave me to keep, asking me to delete from them the passages you had marked, I shall hasten to finish this work and shall return the diaries to you immediately thereafter."[1] Some such action as this may explain the disappearance of his letters to and from Alexandra Tolstoy in 1866, the guarded nature of his entries concerning Ovsiannikov's visit in 1889, and the absence of any other diary mention of the Shabunin affair until 1908. It also seems likely that in their diaries and memoirs his relatives and friends made some effort not to betray his confidence when in conversation he lifted the veil that masked his innermost thoughts. Otherwise I cannot explain why his first known discussion of the case (not counting his talks with Ovsiannikov) apparently occurred as late

The Church Strikes Back

as the summer of 1901—after *Resurrection* and thirty-five years after the event.

The story is told in the diary of the young pianist and composer Alexander Goldenweizer, who later became a professor at the Moscow Conservatory and for a time its principal. Goldenweizer was only twenty years old when he met the Tolstoys, in early 1896, but he soon became an intimate friend. He called on them in their Moscow home and often visited Yasnaya Polyana, where he frequently entertained the family by playing duets with Sonya's composer friend, Taneyev. And when *Resurrection* was being readied for publication, he joined Sonya and several of the children in correcting the proofs and making them conform to Tolstoy's numerous revisions.

There was no such work to be done, however, when he arrived at Yasnaya Polyana in the summer of 1901. His was a social visit, primarily to see Tatyana, who was staying with her mother and father. Suddenly one evening—it was the nineteenth of June—Tolstoy for no known reason began to speak of the Shabunin affair. I say "for no known reason" because Goldenweizer, perhaps to protect Tolstoy, does not say how the subject came up, whether they were talking about the editor Mikhail Stasyulevich and someone mentioned his younger brother or whether Tolstoy was reminded of the younger brother because he was writing *Hadji Murad*, the memorable story of the Caucasian chieftain who was killed after deserting first the cause of the mountain tribesmen, then that of the Russians. Goldenweizer enters abruptly upon Tolstoy's recollections:

June 20, Yasnaya Polyana
This is my fourth day here. Leo Nikolayevich is working a lot on an article, *What the Working People Need*. He also is working on *Hadji Murad* and has asked me to find for him in Moscow some book with a portrait of Hadji Murad.

The Enigmatic Years

Last evening Leo Nikolayevich told me about [Mikhail] Stasyulevich's brother.

Then, quoting Tolstoy directly:

"When he was 18–20 years old, he [Alexander] was a guards officer. They assigned him to security duty at a jail and unfortunately while he was on duty someone escaped. Nikolai Pavolvich [Nicholas I] ordered him reduced to the ranks and exiled him to the Caucasus. [This version does not correspond with the facts as recorded in Tolstoy's diary in 1853, but it is evidently how he recalled them forty-seven years later.] I partly described him in the tale *Meeting a Moscow Acquaintance in the Detachment*. I did not do it well. He was so pitiful. I should not have tried to describe him. However, it was not entirely he. I merged him with [Nikolai] Kashkin, who was tried [convicted and sent for a soldier] with Dostoyevsky.

"Despite all the petitions of relatives and friends, Nikolai Pavlovich did not pardon him. Later on, under Alexander [II], he was pardoned, became an army officer, and served in Tula. Stasyulevich never succeeded in extricating himself from his difficult position. His brother [Mikhail] treated him coldly and with disapproval. In the end Stasyulevich took his own life. He put on a raccoon coat and, wearing the coat, threw himself into the water and drowned.

"When there occurred in Tula the incident about the scribe who slapped an officer who was harassing him, Stasyulevich came and asked me to defend this unfortunate man at the court-martial. I agreed and went. Yunosha was the president. He had two votes and the [other] judges —Grisha Kolokoltsov and Stasyulevich—one each. Stasyulevich voted for acquittal. The two votes of the president were cast for conviction. Everything depended on Kolokoltsov. And suddenly this dear Grisha Kolokoltsov declared for conviction.

"They sentenced the scribe to death. I interceded in Petersburg. Alexandra Andreyevna [Tolstoy] at that time was the tutor of Alexander II's children. I wrote her and she went to see Milyutin. Milyutin alleged I had not designated the regiment, although nothing prevented him from asking which regiment was in Tula. That was only an excuse. The real reason was that not long before at another place there had been a slap-in-the-face incident, and they decided to be very strict. So they shot the unfortunate man."[2]

An intriguing recollection, most noteworthy because it indicates Tolstoy did not suspect that the army had rigged the case against Shabunin and because of the cursory, cool, and matter-of-fact manner in which Tolstoy told his hazy story. One senses that Goldenweizer and anyone else who was present knew Tolstoy was in an unusually confiding mood that evening and not to be pushed into saying more than he wished, for to judge from the diary entry, no one asked what action Tolstoy took when he heard of Milyutin's attitude, no one asked how he heard Shabunin would be shot, no one asked whether he made a last-minute effort to stay the execution, no one asked whether he stood there in the field, saw Shabunin strapped to the stake, heard the command to fire. No one, it seems, asked whether what happened that morning had anything to do with his crusade against church and state. But whether it did or not, by the time of this discussion matters had passed the breaking point, because four months before, on February 22, Tolstoy was excommunicated by order of the Holy Synod (with state connivance).

Tolstoy had probably seen it coming. As early as 1886, high churchmen had denounced him as a heretic and infidel. When he was active in famine relief in 1892, priests urged starving peasants not to accept his bread. In 1896, Konstantin Pobedonostsev, procurator of the Holy Synod, urged the tsar to incarcerate him in one of the dreaded cells at Suzdal monastery, and in 1899 excommunication was formally proposed and rejected.[3] After *Resurrection*, however, church and state could bear the strain no longer. They could survive the devil and all his works and had done so for a thousand years, but the fiercely invective pen of Leo Tolstoy was too much. When he jumped to the defense of students in Kiev who were sentenced to the army for disturbing the peace, retaliation was swift. Pobedonostsev drafted the edict, which was signed by seven churchmen, including three metropolitans, a rank above that of archbishop and below that of patriarch:

> God has permitted a new false teacher to appear—Count Leo Tolstoy. Well known to the world as a writer, Russian by birth, Orthodox by baptism and education, Count Tolstoy, seduced by intellectual pride, has arrogantly risen against the Lord and His Christ and His holy heritage, and has plainly in the sight of all repudiated his Orthodox Mother Church which reared and educated him, and has dedicated his literary activity and the talent given to him by God to disseminating among the people teaching opposed to Christ and the Church, and to destroying in the minds and hearts of people their national faith, that Orthodox faith which has been confirmed by the universe, and in which our forefathers lived and were saved, and to which Holy Russia till now has clung, and in which it has been strong. In his works and letters, distributed in great numbers by him and his followers throughout the world, and particularly within the borders of our dear land, he preaches with zealous fanaticism the overthrow of all the dogmas of the Orthodox Church and the very essence of the Christian faith.

It was said that he denied God, that he refuted Jesus Christ, that he did not accept the Immaculate Conception of the Virgin Mary, that he did not believe in the life hereafter or in judgment after death, that he had mocked the Holy Eucharist.

"Therefore," the edict concluded, "the Church does not reckon him as its member and cannot so reckon him until he repents and resumes his communion with her."[4]

Tolstoy replied on April 4 in a letter that was printed widely in England but in Russia only in the official *Church Gazette* and two unofficial church publications, and in censored form at that. Clearly it was not an exposition that church and state wished to be read by millions of the faithful.

"I believe in this," Tolstoy wrote in part.

I believe in God, whom I understand as Spirit, as love, as the Source of all. I believe He is in me and I in Him. I believe that the will of God is most clearly and intelligibly expressed in the teaching of the man Jesus, whom to consider as God and pray to, I esteem the greatest blasphemy. I believe that man's true welfare lies in fulfilling God's will, and His will is that men should love one another and should consequently do to others as they wish others to do to them—of which it is said in the Gospels that in this is the law and the prophets. I believe, therefore, that the meaning of the life of every man is to be found only in increasing the love that is in him; that this increase of love leads man, even in this life, to ever greater and greater blessedness, and after death gives him more blessedness the more love he has, and helps more than anything else towards the establishment of the Kingdom of God on earth: that is, to the establishment of an order of life in which the discord, deception and violence that now rule will be replaced by free accord, by truth, and by the brotherly love of one for another.

He ended with these words:

Whether or not these beliefs of mine offend, grieve, or prove a stumbling block to anyone, or hinder anything, or give displeasure to anybody, I can as little change them as I can change my body. I must myself live my own life, and I must myself alone meet death (and that very soon), and therefore I cannot believe otherwise than as I—preparing to go to that God from whom I came—do believe. I do not believe my faith to be the one indubitable truth for all time, but I see no other that is plainer, clearer, or answers better to all the demands of my reason and my heart; should I find such a one I shall at once accept it; for God requires nothing but the truth. But I can no more return to that from which with such suffering I have escaped, than a flying bird can re-enter the eggshell from which it has emerged.[5]

Now it was a fight to the finish between the church, which from long experience understood how dangerous to itself such thoughts could be, and Tolstoy, who would not repent even on his deathbed in 1910; and once again with Sonya, still a devout Orthodox, in the van, the family closed ranks. Tolstoy's wife and children stood by him, as did many friends and thousands of strangers, some of whom hailed and cheered him in the streets of Moscow despite the fact that a copy of the edict that separated him from the church was posted on every church door. Even many people who disagreed with him defended his right to write and speak according to the dictates of his conscience.

Such was the situation when Goldenweizer visited Yasnaya Polyana in the summer of 1901, and such it was in September when Tolstoy, much weakened by a bout with malaria, left on doctor's orders for the milder climate of the Crimea and the Black Sea coast.

13

The Bar Strikes Back

On July 19, 1901, a month after Tolstoy spoke to Goldenweizer "about Stasyulevich's brother," Sonya wrote to Biryukov, who was still in exile but had left England for Switzerland. In Switzerland he had been approached by a French publisher, who was interested in a biography of Tolstoy. Knowing that if she opposed the project, he might as well forget it, Biryukov had asked her permission. Sonya graciously gave her consent.

"Of course it would be a good thing for you to work on a biography," she said in reply, "and Lev Nikolayevich could answer much that you ask of me; only hurry. His dear life almost left us all. But now, glory be to God, Lev Nikolayevich is recovering and again working well."[1] (She referred to a persistent fever he ran in March and April, but wrote before an attack of malaria that would drive him to the Crimea in the fall.)

Not wishing to trouble Tolstoy at this time and believing he would have no objections anyway, Biryukov accepted the assignment and set to work. In late autumn, however, he realized he needed help and wrote to the Crimea, where the ailing Tolstoy was in frequent company with two ailing friends, Maxim Gorky, who had been released from prison in May (he had been convicted of possession of an illegal or unauthorized printing press) after Tolstoy interceded on his behalf, and Anton Chekhov, who was dying slowly of tuberculosis. Biryukov asked Tolstoy to sit for a word picture as he had sat for several painters and sculptors, and Tolstoy readily agreed. "I shall be very happy to pose for you and shall answer your questions categorically," he replied on December 2.[2]

Thereafter the two men exchanged many letters, and Tolstoy evidently gave a lot of thought to the matter, for early in 1902 he promised to contribute his recollections, then seemed to back off, then agreed. Something apparently troubled him. It was as if he wanted to tell all—or wanted Biryukov to think he was telling all—yet was reluctant to do so. In May, about a month before he left the Crimea to return to Yasnaya Polyana (he was seriously ill much of the time he was away), he indicated the nature of the problem.

> At first I thought I would not be in a position to help you with my biography in spite of my wish to do so. I feared the insincerity incidental to every biography, but now I seem to have found the form in which I can satisfy your wish, pointing out the main character of the consecutive periods of my life in childhood, youth, and maturity one after the other. As soon as I recover so that I am in a position to write, I will devote some hours to this without fail and try to do it.[3]

He feared "the insincerity incidental to every autobiography"? With good reason. There were matters he would not reveal, as he made plain three months later in another letter to Biryukov. As usual, he called him Posha, the Russian diminutive of Pavel.:

Yasnaya Polyana, August 20, 1902

My dear friend Posha,
    I haven't written to you for ages and ages, and this distresses me very much; it's as if our connection with each

other is getting more distant and tenuous. And this hurts me, because you are one of my closest and best friends who have given me much joy and support. So don't let our connection be broken, not for anything. I'm afraid I mistakenly encouraged you by my promise to write my reminiscences. I tried to think about it, and saw what terrible difficulty there would be in avoiding the Charybdis of self-praise (by keeping silent about everything bad) and the Scylla of cynical frankness about all the vileness of my life. To write down all one's nastiness, stupidity, meanness and depravity quite truthfully—more truthfully even than Rousseau—would make a corrupting book or article. People will say: there's a man whom many people rate highly, and look what a scoundrel he was! So we ordinary people cannot be blamed for doing what he does. Seriously, when I began to recall all my life carefully and saw all its stupidity (actually stupidity) and vileness, I thought: what must other people be like, if I who am praised by many am such a stupid beast? However, I suppose, this could be explained again by the fact that I'm only more crafty than other people. I say all this to you, not for stylistic effect, but completely sincerely. I've lived through it all.

He had lived through all what? Tolstoy did not say, but he closed his letter with a favorable decision that seemed to betray his thinking in the matter:

I said that I'm afraid of a false promise about my reminiscences. I *am* afraid, but that doesn't mean that I refuse. I'll try, when I have more strength and time. I have a plan for avoiding the difficulties I spoke of by only hinting at good and bad periods. Goodbye. I kiss you.

L. T.[4]

One of the "bad periods" may have been the Shabunin affair, which he had never mentioned to Biryukov, although he had known him since 1884.

In the end, Tolstoy did contribute his reminiscences

(largely confined to his family background, recollections of childhood, and answers to specific questions), but in the foreword he wrote for Biryukov's first volume he further obscured the Shabunin case by breaking down his life into four periods and describing the third (from his marriage in 1862 through the execution in 1866 to his "spiritual birth" in the 1870s) as follows: "a period, which, from the worldly point of view, one might call moral; I mean that during these eighteen years I lived a regular, honest family life, without addicting myself to any vices condemned by public opinion, but a period all the interests of which were limited to egotistical family cares, to concern for the increase of wealth, the attainment of literary success, and the enjoyment of every kind of pleasure." He implied he was concealing nothing. He understood, he wrote, that his biography, if written as biographies generally are, "if it passed over in silence all the abomination and criminality of my life, would be a lie, and that, when a man writes his life, he should write the whole and the exact truth. Only such an autobiography, however humiliating it may be for me to write it, can have a true and fruitful interest for the readers."

Tolstoy continued:

> Such a history of my life during all these four periods I should like to write quite, quite truthfully, if God will give me the power and the time. I think that such an autobiography, even though very defective, would be more profitable to men than all that artistic prattle with which the twelve volumes of my works are filled, and to which men of our time attribute an undeserved significance.
>
> And I should now like to do this. I will begin by describing the first joyful period of my childhood, which attracts me with special force; then, however ashamed I may be to do so, I will also describe, without hiding anything, those dreadful twenty years of the following period; then the third period, which may be of the least interest of all.[5]

The Bar Strikes Back

Unfortunately for Tolstoy, it was precisely the "third period" to which the organized legal profession turned its attention in the summer of 1903. Suffering from the contempt and ridicule piled upon them in *Resurrection,* eager to strike back on the occasion of Tolstoy's seventy-fifth birthday, men who practiced at the bar or taught law at the University of St. Petersburg sought some means of pitching him from the perch to which his works and ideas had elevated him. But what was to be done? How to reach him? *Look into his past; see what the army has; talk to the police.* And because there was a will, a way was found. Tolstoy, they learned, had once pleaded the cause of a soldier and lost, and as a consequence the soldier was shot. Why not hold *him* up to ridicule and contempt? Why not attribute his attitude toward courts, judges, lawyers, and the law to the bitterness of personal failure?

And so it happened that on Sunday, August 24, four days before his birthday, *Pravo,* a newspaper edited by seven professors and assistant professors of law, revived the Shabunin affair in an article that filled the front page and more than three inside pages of the tabloid-size weekly.[6] It was written by one M. I. Ippolitov, who somehow got hold of a copy of the Tula paper that had printed Tolstoy's plea to the court in 1866. Behind an unctuous screen of feigned objectivity, with patently ironic references to "the great artist" and "the beloved man," Ippolitov wrote as if with sympathy and understanding. His thinly veiled point, however, was that Tolstoy had made a mess of the case from opening to closing gavel. In an exposition from which one may infer that he, too, knew nothing of the Moscow file, Ippolitov called Tolstoy's plea *advokatski*—routinely lawyer-like.

These days when the Russian land is preparing to celebrate solemnly the 75th birthday of its great writer, interest in everything about his personality and creative work reaches a special degree of intensity. At such a moment his entire life—even an insignificant fact—his every word, if unknown to the reader, is precious, as is precious a new touch, a new shading [of the painter's brush], that reveals an aspect of the beloved man.

The page from the life of L. N. Tolstoy that we are able to make known to our readers is, it seems, unknown to biographer and critic, but to our way of thinking an anniversary frame of mind is not needed to justify it. It is of interest in itself and has unquestioned significance for an understanding of Tolstoy's attitude toward the phenomena of justice.

Tolstoy first dealt with a court of law and judicial procedure in *War and Peace*. There is no need for us to recall the trial of Pierre Bezukhov. His [Tolstoy's] indignation at a system that is trying to get at judicial truth is apparent. You remember he likens the system to a groove that leads to conviction and into which fall only those things the authorities wish to fall. The reader certainly will recall that it concerns not only a court-martial operating in a city occupied by the enemy [the French], but all courts— and with what blood-curdling detail the scene is described when the last bloody act of this judicial procedure is performed—the shooting of the accused. An indignant humane spirit bursts forth in every line of such scenes.

In Tolstoy's subsequent works, for a long time one does not encounter images and pictures of the legal world, but the spirit of hostility to a court of law remains; in *Resurrection* it is cultivated, deepened, and gushes like a stream. We are not one of those jurists who saw in the novel nothing but slander of the activity of jurists. On the contrary, we think the problem of crime and punishment is posed nakedly in its moral essence, that it lays bare the real truth, and that this truth does not suffer from the social perspective that Tolstoy erroneously injected into it. Judicial critics of *Resurrection* have spoken much about these errors but very little about the essence; they keenly note the hostility that grips the pen of the artist as soon as it is a question of

The Bar Strikes Back

courts of law, the administration of the law, details of court procedure, or anything directly or indirectly associated with them.

Where did this characteristic come from? It is certainly not connected organically with the problem, and it is evident it is not required for artistic elucidation.

Perhaps to answer this question we have to explore the sensations Tolstoy experienced when he had a part in an affair with which we wish to acquaint the reader. The personal life, the personal feelings, of an artist often best explain his works, and in our time especially [literary] criticism emphasizes the association. Tolstoy's personal life was always a mighty spring from which by the power of his genius he scooped images, thoughts, and ideas he transformed into artistic works, intelligible to us all.

One senses that Ippolitov, having set the stage, is about to draw the sword. The weapon glitters in a heavy hand that trembles in his eagerness.

Evidently Tolstoy first collided with questions about crime and the law in the Shabunin affair with which we are concerned, and this new field, affecting the artist in its most terrible form, must have left an ineradicable furrow in the soul of the artist. So far as one may judge from the plea published below, Tolstoy assumed the defense of this unfortunate little soldier [*soldatik*] without reflecting deeply on these questions. All the arguments in his plea revolve within conventional limits and patterns. Tolstoy is concerned with interpreting the law, comparing articles of the law; he talks about the general spirit of our legislation, about irresponsibility, and so on. Tolstoy's plea is totally *advokatski* in character; he tries to follow the superficial format of pleading. Coming from the mouth of Tolstoy, the author of *Resurrection*, how strange the plea sounds to us now!

147

The Enigmatic Years

Strange, indeed, because Tolstoy's thinking had changed considerably over the years. But one wonders what Ippolitov would have said to the court in 1866. Did he think he would have succeeded where Tolstoy failed? He continued:

> After that affair Tolstoy could hardly have preserved his former attitude toward the law. A brutal act, rare in the annals of jurisprudence [it was not so rare as Ippolitov pretended to think], was committed. For striking an officer, a drunken little soldier [Ippolitov apparently was pleased with his contemptuous characterization of Shabunin] is condemned to death. The penalty is exacted—perhaps before the eyes of his defender—and an ordinary man, one not dried up by the practice of law, was bound to be deeply shocked. How did it affect the sensitive psyche of the artist? The image of Shabunin, condemned to be shot by the judgment of a court, had to cut deeply into his memory and heart, Tolstoy says somewhere [*Confession*] that the first death penalty he witnessed abroad caused him to question the values of European progress. . . . Given the fact that at Shabunin's punishment Tolstoy was not a mere spectator—he tried to save his life—he lived through all the brutality and senselessness of what occurred. Perhaps the image of Shabunin stood before the great artist when, with the impression fresh, he described the scene of Pierre's court-martial and the shocking details of the execution scene.
>
> Let us move on, however, to the facts we found in a totally forgotten sheet published in Tula in 1866.

There followed a short account of the incident, the text of Tolstoy's plea, the guilty verdict, and a few lines about the execution, but Ippolitov reserved for himself the final paragraph: "Apparently Tolstoy's plea on behalf of the defense passed without notice in the newspapers. Only the landlords' *News* praised the speech, finding it distinguished by the absence of resourcefulness and by the conformity to law of its viewpoint."

A mean story and intended to be, but apparently it missed its mark, for Ippolitov's article, like Tolstoy's plea, passed unnoticed by the newspapers of the day, possibly because it was blocked by the state's censors or because their editors considered it a blow below the belt at a time when from all over the world letters, telegrams, and resolutions of birthday congratulations were flowing into Yasnaya Polyana. Tolstoy received a copy without mentioning it in his diary (unless the entry was later destroyed) or writing about it to friends (unless the copies of the letters were also destroyed). As for Biryukov, uninformed of the *Pravo* attack, he continued to work in exile on the first volume of his biography, still believing that the "third period" of Tolstoy's life was of "the least interest of all."

Questions. Questions. Didn't Mikhail Stasyulevich in St. Petersburg read the article and write Tolstoy about it? Apparently not, perhaps because Tolstoy had never told him his brother was involved in the case, perhaps because Ippolitov did not use Alexander's name and Mikhail did not see the connection. Didn't Tolstoy's friend Koni, who gave him the idea for *Resurrection*, clip the story and send it on to Yasnaya Polyana with a covering letter? Apparently not. Didn't Tolstoy's other jurist friend Nikolai Davydov, a lecturer in law at the University of Moscow, whom Tolstoy consulted about *Resurrection*, write him about it? It seems not. To judge from the surviving record, either *Pravo's* bombshell bombed or Tolstoy's family and friends intentionally ignored it.

In the event, the enigmatic years might have remained forever more enigmatic than they are if Tolstoy had not filed a copy quietly away among the letters, papers, notes, and other documents that cluttered his study and closets.

PART THREE

Tolstoy Breaks Silence

That incident had much more influence on my life than all the seemingly more important events of life: the loss of or recovery of wealth, successes or failures in literature, even the loss of people close to me.

—Tolstoy to Biryukov, May 24, 1908

14

Enter Biryukov

It would be difficult to imagine a more conscientious man than Pavel Biryukov. In strict adherence to moral principles there were not many men like him in his day, as there are few in ours. He tried to do what he thought he ought to do, and so far as I can tell, in working toward that goal he never wavered, even if that meant occasional and strong disagreement with Tolstoy.

As a young man, Biryukov easily entered the *corps de pages* in St. Petersburg, which was a powerful springboard for the sons of aristocratic families. A graduate of the *corps de pages*, he just as easily entered the Naval Academy, which, if he kept out of trouble, guaranteed social prominence and access later on to the court and imperial family. Biryukov, however, was made of unusual stuff. As a midshipman he had sailed around the world and accompanied one of the grand dukes on a voyage to Palestine, but by the time he got his commission in 1884 he realized that military service was not for him. Religious by nature, having come to believe that war was murder, he left the navy, sought out Chertkov, the former Guards officer who shared Tolstoy's views about nonviolence, and joined Tolstoy for life, except for a few brief periods when he lived on his family estate at Kostroma, managing it as best he could. Exiled in 1897 along with

Tolstoy Breaks Silence

Chertkov and Tregubov—"for my religious opinions," as he said, "a senseless administrative order"[1]—he eagerly took on the task of writing Tolstoy's biography in 1901, but it is my notion that by the fall of 1903 he was worrying about his ability to finish it. He had asked the ministry of internal affairs for permission to return to Russia for two months so that he might talk to the Tolstoys and go over Leo's papers. Permission denied. He had traveled from Geneva to London to interview Chertkov and search out material in the Russian department of the British Museum. He had written to many of Tolstoy's friends and acquaintances and asked them to contribute anything that might be of interest. Still he had reason to think Tolstoy was finding it hard to accommodate him. The reminiscences were beginning to come in and Tolstoy was stronger now than he had been in 1901 and 1902, going for long horseback rides and playing tennis, but he had other concerns than the biography. Much as he wished to help Biryukov—he enjoyed recalling his youth—he had only a limited fund of nervous energy, and he was constantly drawing on it. He was writing compulsively, as if he had not much time to live, as he seriously believed. In August he finished *After the Ball*, the story of the soldier who is beaten to death as he walks the gauntlet; he then returned to *Hadji Murad*, his last novel, which he would complete the following year. He had other problems—with Sonya, as so often; with several of his sons, who disagreed with him about almost everything; with himself, because of men sent to prison or disciplinary battalions for refusing military service or for distributing his forbidden works. One problem that troubled him, as it had for some years now, was a conviction that Russia was headed for revolution and war. He was as sure of this last belief as he was that fall would follow summer and winter follow fall. And to one who is aware of the course of human events there are few matters more frustrating, more agonizing, than to foresee disaster and be unable to prevent it. He had tried for twenty years. He had tried most earnestly in a well-known letter to young Nicholas II, which he wrote from Gaspra, in the Crimea, on January 16, 1902.

Dear Brother.

I consider this form of address to be most appropriate because I address you in this letter not so much as a tsar but as a man—a brother—and furthermore because I am writing to you as it were from the next world, since I expect to die very soon.

I did not want to die without telling you what I think of your present activity, of what it could be, of what great good it could bring to millions of people and to yourself, and of what great evil it can bring to those people and to yourself if it continues in the same direction in which it is now going.

A third of Russia is in a state of emergency, i.e. outside the law. The army of police—open and secret—is constantly growing. Over and above the hundreds of thousands of criminals, the prisons, the places of exile, and labor camps are overflowing with political prisoners, to whom workers are now being added as well. The censorship has descended to nonsensical prohibitions, which it never descended to in the worst period of the '40s [under Nicholas I]. Religious persecutions were never so frequent and cruel as they are now, and they are becoming more and more cruel and frequent. Armed forces are concentrated everywhere in the cities and industrial centers and are sent out against the people with live cartridges. In many places there has already been bloodshed between brothers, and further and more cruel bloodshed is imminent everywhere and will inevitably follow.

Tolstoy said the people were becoming more impoverished every year and that famine had become "a normal occurrence." He continued:

Tolstoy Breaks Silence

There is one cause of all this and it is manifestly evident: namely that your aides assure you that by halting any movement of life among the people they are thereby ensuring the well-being of the people and your own peace and security. But one can far more easily halt a river's flow than halt mankind's continual progress forward as ordained by God.

He challenged Orthodoxy and autocracy as "a double falsehood." People no longer believed, he said, that the tsar was an "infallible God on earth."

Autocracy is an obsolete form of government which may suit the needs of a people somewhere in Central Africa, cut off from the whole world, but not the needs of the Russian people who are becoming more and more enlightened by the enlightenment common to the whole world. And therefore maintaining this form of government and the Orthodoxy linked with it can only be done as it is now, by means of every kind of violence: a state of emergency, administrative exile, executions, religious persecutions, the banning of books and newspapers, the perversion of education, and, in general, by bad and cruel actions of every type.

Such have been the actions of your reign up to now. Starting with your reply to the Tver [Kalinin] deputation which roused the indignation of all Russian society by calling the legitimate desires of the people "foolish daydreams"—all your decrees about Finland [obliging the Finns to do military service in the Russian army] and the seizure of Chinese territories [the forced partition of Chinese territory by which the Russians gained a lease on the ice-free harbor at Port Arthur], your Hague Conference project [called by Nicholas to limit military expenditures by international agreement] accompanied by the strengthening of the army, your weakening of self-government and strengthening of administrative arbitrariness, your support of religious persecutions, your consent to the establishment of a monopoly on spirits, i.e. government traffic in poison for the people, and finally your obstinacy in maintaining corporal punishment despite all the representations made to you for the abolition of this senseless and entirely useless measure, humiliating to the Russian people—all these are actions which you could have avoided taking, had you not set yourself, on the advice of your frivolous aides, an impossible goal—not only to halt the people's life, but to return it to a former obsolete state.

Tolstoy then gave the tsar some positive advice:

The people can be oppressed by violent measures, but they cannot be governed by them. The only means of effectively governing the people in our time is to head the people's movement from evil to goodness, from darkness to light, and to lead them to the attainment of the goals nearest to it. In order to be able to do this, it is necessary first of all to give the people the opportunity to express their wishes and needs and, having heard these wishes and needs, to fulfill those of them which will answer the needs, not of one class or estate but of the majority, the mass of the working people.

Words rarely heard by a tsar, but words from the heart. Tolstoy concluded:

Think about this, not in the presence of people, but in the presence of God, and do what God, i.e., your conscience, tells you. And don't be troubled by the obstacles you will encounter if you enter on a new path in life. These obstacles will be eliminated of their own accord and you will not notice them, if only what you do is done not for human glory, but for your own soul, i.e. for God.

Forgive me if I have unwittingly offended or angered you by what I have written in this letter. I was only guided by a desire for the good of the Russian people and of yourself. Whether I have accomplished this will be decided by the future, which I, in all probability, will not see. I have done what I considered my duty.[2]

Needless to say, Tolstoy did not accomplish his purpose, nor did he live to see the last act in the revolutionary struggle that would be played out in 1917, but he looked sadly on while it raged throughout 1903, reached a crisis in 1904, and passed a point of no return with the revolution of 1905. Nicholas did not answer Tolstoy's letter. A weak man, unable to control the men around him, almost a captive of his wife and reactionary officials who believed the only language the people understood was force, he sailed on as if the ship of state were headed for safe harbor, but the winds blew and the rains came, and he never seemed to understand why. It is almost certain he did not understand that a pogrom in Kishinev that lasted for three days in April 1903 (an act that led to the formation in the United States of the American Jewish Committee) was state-tolerated if not state-inspired. Hate ran amuck in Kishinev. Some fifty Jews were killed. Hundreds were wounded. While army troops were kept in their barracks and the police stood indifferently by, more than a thousand homes and shops were destroyed. The "culprit," Tolstoy wrote to the writer Sholom Aleichem, who organized a fund to aid the victims, was "the government," and he promptly added his name to a general telegram of protest that was addressed to the governor of the town: "Profoundly shocked by the atrocities committed at Kishinev, we extend our heartfelt sympathy to the innocent victims of mob savagery and express our horror at the acts of cruelty perpetrated by Russians, our scorn and disgust with all who have driven the people to such a pass and have allowed this dreadful crime to be committed."[3]

Biryukov, in far-off Geneva, and Chertkov, in far-off England, were similarly stunned by what was going on in their homeland. Things went from bad to worse, with the Japanese sneak attack on the Russian fleet in Port Arthur in early 1904, followed by a Japanese invasion of Russian-held territory across the Yalu in May. Having allowed his country to slip into a war he could not win, forced to fight at the end of the uncompleted Trans-Siberian Railway, Nicholas sought to make the best of it, but as the first wave of patriotic fervor waned (Tolstoy's son Andrei left home to join the army in February), protests mounted from those who demanded victory and those who espoused nonviolence. In May, Tolstoy wrote an article, *Bethink Yourselves,* published in England, which condemned both sides in the war. On June 3, Nikolai Bobrikov, the governor general of Finland, was shot to death by a student. On July 16, Vyasheslav Pleve, the minister of internal affairs, was killed when students threw a bomb under his carriage. For Biryukov and his biography, however, there were two favorable developments that year. In February, Sonya went to Moscow and succeeded in persuading the authorities to set aside a room in the Historical Museum on Red Square for Tolstoy's manuscripts, letters, and other papers. And late that summer, to celebrate the birth of his son and heir, Alexis, on July 30, Nicholas declared a limited amnesty for some political offenders. Biryukov (and later Chertkov) was among them, as he explained in a postscript to his preface to Volume 1:

> I had already reached the end of my first volume, when, in consequence of a temporary relaxation of repressive measures in Russia, I received permission to revisit my country. I went to Russia, accordingly, and have there been able adequately to enlarge the biographical material of the first volume, thanks to my personal intercourse with Tolstoy himself, and also by reading his diaries and correspondence, for which privilege I am deeply grateful to

Tolstoy Breaks Silence

Countess S. Tolstoy. She gave me access to the valuable collections of biographical materials collected by her and placed in the Historical Museum of Moscow, in the room called after Tolstoy's name.[4]

That trip helped so much that although Biryukov wrote the preface on October 15, 1904, he dated the postscript August 23, 1905; after he had "reached the end of" his first volume, then, he still had ten months of work ahead of him.

And for Biryukov that was the easy period of Tolstoy's life, from his birth, in 1828, through his marriage, in 1862. The trouble would come when he turned to the years from 1862 to 1884. "In the second volume," he wrote in the preface to the first, "will be described the period of Tolstoy's greatest literary success, family happiness, and material welfare, followed by an important crisis which led to his birth into a new spiritual life."[5] Little he knew of the shock that awaited him.

15

The Telltale File

About the time Biryukov's first volume came out, in 1906 (he was not happy with it but it was the best he could do under the circumstances), another friend and worker on Tolstoy's behalf who was writing a biography of his own arrived at Yasnaya Polyana. He was an Englishman, Aylmer Maude, who had first gone to Russia in 1874 and stayed twenty-three years. He had married an Englishwoman, Louise Shanks, who was also living in Moscow. They returned home in 1897, not long after Biryukov and Chertkov were exiled from their native land. Between 1897 and 1906 Maude traveled to Canada to aid in the resettlement of the Dukhobors, wrote a book titled *Tolstoy and His Problems* and another on the Dukhobors, and quarreled from time to time with Chertkov, once over the copyright to Louise Maude's translation into English of *Resurrection,* which Chertkov thought should be surrendered in line with Tolstoy's long-held policy. Maude also had a few unpleasant things to say about Biryukov's allegedly naive perception of the Dukhobor movement in 1895, but he was sincere in his attachment to Tolstoy and Sonya and viewed the disputes between them in a light more favorable to her than was the case with most of Tolstoy's followers. So from 1906 on there were rival biographers in and out of Yasnaya Polyana, both helped by Tolstoy and also by his wife, though only up to a point, for neither one intended to tell all. To be specific, neither one proposed to tell about the Shabunin affair, a subject that for forty years had rarely been mentioned outside of the intimate family circle, except, it seems, in serious talk with such men as Goldenweizer, whose discretion could be relied on.

Would one of his biographers get the story? Would he tell it if he got it, or regard its disclosure as something of an intrusion on a man's private life? There was a chance. Tolstoy had referred to the case in conversation with Goldenweizer on June 19, 1901, and the record reveals he also referred to it on June 8, 1905, in the presence of Dr. Dushan Makovitsky, a Slovak physician and earnest Tolstoyan, who had taken up residence with the family the preceding December. As in his meetings with Ovsiannikov in 1889 and his talk with Goldenweizer in 1901, however, not everything he said on this occasion or why he said it is known. Indeed, all we have is one tantalizing sentence, apparently scratched out by Makovitsky, who was in the habit of keeping his right hand in his pocket, where a pencil and small notebook were concealed, to preserve without Tolstoy's knowledge a quotable Tolstoy remark. The sentence reads: "It was a good thing that during my plea I burst into tears."[1]

So he cried before the court and remembered he cried. One wonders at which point in his plea he "burst into tears," and why it was "a good thing." Because he knew or felt that that display of emotion had helped to sway Stasyulevich's vote?

More consequentially, one wonders, as with Goldenweizer, how the subject came up. Was it because Makovitsky happened to say he was born in 1866 and the year clicked in Tolstoy's mind? Or because, while talking of death and the death penalty, he uncharacteristically felt the need to unburden his soul? It is impossible to say, although for Tolstoy the past year had been exceptionally painful and distressing. On March 21, 1904, his beloved cousin Alexandra, who had tried to help him in 1866, died in St. Petersburg at the age of eighty-seven. In August he hurried over to Pirogovo in time to see his only surviving brother, Sergei, before Sergei died of cancer on the twenty-third. Or did Tolstoy raise the subject because he was unusually despondent? If he was, he had reason to be. On January 2, 1905, Port Arthur fell to the Japanese. A week later, on Bloody Sunday, as it is called, hundreds were killed in St. Petersburg when troops opened fire on workers who were marching on the Winter Palace to petition the tsar for civil rights. (Sonya's older brother Alexander, Kolokoltsov's friend, was there with his regiment that day; Tolstoy's friend Gorky was also there—on the other side.) On February 5 the grand duke Sergei, the tsar's uncle, was assassinated in Moscow. In March the Japanese took Mukden, in distant Manchuria, and in May, in the Tsushima Strait in the Far East, they destroyed a Russian fleet that had left the Baltic in October. In sum, when Tolstoy spoke in Makovitsky's presence, Russia was in turmoil. Revolutionary activity and police repression were everyday occurrences, both matters of burning concern to Russia's apostle of nonviolence.

Yet clearly how the subject came up is of less significance than that it came up, for his speaking of the affair at all suggests that he was still thinking and worrying about the fact that possibly because of some fault of his a young soldier was blindfolded, strapped to a stake, and cut down by sharpshooters. How much longer could he conceal the episode from his biographers?

Nineteen-six was an increasingly difficult year. There was mounting political opposition to the regime. Revolutionaries intensified their terrorist activity. Public hangings were becoming commonplace.

In July, Tolstoy got into a nasty argument with his sons Leo and Andrei, who believed in capital punishment. This was too much for the old man. "I told them that they did not respect me," he wrote to his daughter Marya, "that they hated me, and I slammed the door as I left the room, and for a couple of days I could not come to my senses."[2]

In August, Prime Minister Peter Stolypin's summer house was blown up. Twenty-seven persons were killed. Stolypin's daughter was injured.

On November 26, Marya died of double pneumonia. Tolstoy followed the coffin to the cemetery gate but could not bring himself to go farther.

And sometime during that year Maude asked Tolstoy about the Shabunin affair. How he heard of it is uncertain; perhaps from Ovsiannikov's article, which had been published before he left Russia in 1897, perhaps while he was in England from someone who had read *Pravo* in 1903.

Tolstoy brushed the question aside, casually, as if with indifference. Says Maude in his first volume, *The Life of Tolstoy: First Fifty Years*: "Tolstoy, when telling me of the incident, remarked that of the four occasions on which he has spoken in public, this was the time that he did so with the most assurance and satisfaction to himself."[3] Believing him and evidently hearing nothing to the contrary from Sonya, who read over and corrected his manuscript, Maude devoted under three pages to the case.

Biryukov, still unaware of it, wrote on.

In May 1907 Sonya's younger brother Vyacheslav Bers, an engineer, was assassinated by unemployed workers at a factory near St. Petersburg.

During the summer, at Chertkov's suggestion, Tolstoy took on a young secretary, Nikolai Gusev. For alleged subversive activity (working for Tolstoy), Gusev was arrested on October 22. Tolstoy visited him in prison and obtained his release just before Christmas.

Also just before Christmas Tolstoy received a phonograph-dictating machine from its American inventor, Thomas A. Edison.

Maude finished his first volume. Biryukov finished his second.

And so at the dawn of the critical year 1908, Tolstoy and Sonya had reason to think the Shabunin affair was tucked away from the prying eyes of history. Maude's account was cursory; Sonya knew, because she had revised his manuscript "both verbally and in writing."[4] Biryukov, who wrote the preface to his second volume on January 11 and sent it off to the Intermediary, Tolstoy's publishing house, did not speak of it. Before Biryukov, however, loomed months of work on his third volume, which would pick up the story of Tolstoy's life from 1884, and he quickly set to it. Coming from his estate near Kostroma, he arrived at Yasnaya Polyana in the middle of the month and left on the twenty-third, taking with him copies of Tolstoy's letters and diaries and a number of files he would look through at home. He returned on February 2 and left soon after with more documentary material. He came back in March and April.

Undisturbed by these comings and goings, Tolstoy had two causes for anxiety during this period. One was an almost nationwide plan to celebrate his eightieth birthday, August 28; he was determined to stop it, and he did. The other was the increasing number of executions that followed hard upon the revolution of 1905. Furious because of what was going on, he decided to do something about it, and on March 5 wrote for the first time in four years to Mikhail Stasyulevich, asking him to publish a story on the death penalty by the peasant writer Sergei Semenov; Mikhail agreed.[5] And on April 9 he wrote to his jurist friend Nikolai Davydov in Moscow, requesting background material. "I need to know," he said in part, "details about capital punishment, the trial, the sentences and the whole procedure; if you can provide me with the fullest details you will greatly oblige me. My questions are these: who institutes proceedings, how are they conducted, who confirms them, how, where and by whom is the action carried out; how are the gallows constructed, how is the executioner dressed, who is present at the execution."[6]

He needed the material for an article—*I Cannot Be Silent*—which he would write at white heat. Before he got down to it, however, something unexpected and distrubing occurred.

Biryukov turned up at Yasnaya Polyana in what I imagine was a state of extreme agitation. He had come across a file on the Shabunin affair. Though he had known and worked with Tolstoy for twenty-four years, he had never heard of it before. He was horrified—horrified as a man because he could guess at the heavy weight of this silent burden Tolstoy had borne for forty-two years, horrified as a conscientious biographer because he had covered the year 1866 without referring to it in his second volume, which was already in proof form.

There is no record of their meeting or confrontation on this occasion. Evidently, however, Biryukov asked about the file—did it tell a true story?—and evidently Tolstoy instantly understood he could not or should not lie to him. Yes, he said, it had happened as the contents of the file indicated: the testimony of a witness to the scene when Shabunin struck Yasevich, a clipping from the Tula weekly reporting the trial and execution, Ovsiannikov's description of the peasants around the grave site, a copy of the 1903 issue of *Pravo*, and what else I do not know.

But, Biryukov asked, what had it meant to him then? What did it mean to him now? And Tolstoy, I think, broke down, because it would seem that no man can bear such a cross for so long without being deeply moved at the moment of confession or disclosure. I also think the time came when the determined biographer said he could not in good conscience ignore the affair—he would have to include it in his second volume—and Tolstoy understood. If Biryukov would send him an account of the incident based on the Shabunin file, he would comment in the form of a letter in which he would include his recollection of the case and his judgment of its influence on him.

In consequence, Biryukov's account arrived at Yasnaya Polyana in late April, and Tolstoy, with considerable courage, began to write on May 1.[7]

16

Guilt and Remorse

Had Tolstoy fought for Shabunin as persistently as Nekhludov in *Resurrection* fought for Katusha, had he revealed remorse at the time or publicly discussed the case on any occasion thereafter, either orally or in one of his dogmatic works, there would have been no need to write of it in the spring of 1908. Like everyone else, however, he was, as he often said, an imperfect man, and now he was prepared to make what amends he could by baring his soul to foe and friend alike. The effort was intensely dramatic. He began to write in longhand on May 1, turned to dictation (to Gusev) the same day, burst into tears three times in the course of it, and did not finish until the twenty-fourth of the month. In the interim, in short letters that indicate they already knew all about the case, he told Chertkov and Davydov what he was doing, and on the sixth mentioned it in his diary for the first time since he had seen Ovsiannikov in 1889. The reference suggests he was quite pleased with his effort: "I have devoted about four days to recollections about the soldier for Posha. Not too badly, even provocatively [*Ni ochen durno, no sadorno*]."[1] If he had kept a more complete, a more revealing record in this period, the entries would have read something like this:

Guilt and Remorse

May 1. Began letter to Biryukov. Wrote short note to Chertkov to tell him I am writing about the case.[2]

May 2. Continued dictating to Gusev. Revised and made some corrections in early pages of typewritten draft.

May 3. More corrections. Completed draft. Wrote to Davydov, asking him to receive Biryukov in Moscow, look over draft, and make sure it contains no inaccuracies.[3]

May 6. This is my first diary reference to the case in nineteen years.

May 9. Executions, executions, executions, unceasingly! Today's paper reports twenty peasants were hanged in Kherson for an attack on a landowner's estate with intent to rob. A shameful outrage! Began article, *I Cannot Be Silent*.[4]

May 10. Letter from Mikhail Stasyulevich enclosing several copies of *The European Herald*. Thanked him and added I am writing for my biography an account of the case in which his younger brother was involved.

May 11. Hear that on the seventh a St. Petersburg court sentenced Molochnikov to a year in prison for possessing and distributing my forbidden works.

May 12. The well-known lawyer Muraviev was here today. Told him about Molochnikov's case and urged him to help. He agreed.

May 13. Wrote Molochnikov that Muraviev would do everything in his power to help. Started letter to the newspaper *Rus* on the Molochnikov affair.

May 18. Mailed letter to *Rus*.

May 24. Finished letter to Biryukov.

May 31. Finished *I Cannot Be Silent*.

Tolstoy Breaks Silence

Meanwhile, Biryukov, working against a deadline, had sent to the printers, as he had earlier to Tolstoy, his version of the case and a paragraph of comment that would precede Tolstoy's letter when it was ready for publication. As it was too late to rewrite the first four chapters, which dealt with the years 1862–69, he decided to tell the story in a new chapter that would be inserted between the first four and the original Chapter 5. Accordingly, he began with an account of the incident, moved on to the trial, quoted Tolstoy's plea from *Pravo*, and briefly described what happened thereafter. Then, implying both shock at hearing of the affair and continuing respect for and loyalty to Tolstoy, he added this thought as an introduction to Tolstoy's letter:

> A reader who knows and understands Lev Nikolayevich must be left with a feeling of disappointment at the colorless role that Lev Nikolayevich Tolstoi played in this matter. I, too, experienced a feeling of disappointment when I wrote about it with the documents before me. Knowing the attitude of Lev Nikolayevich toward such a terrible phenomenon as capital punishment, I asked him to explain his present attitude toward his participation in the defense of the executed soldier. And with all the sincerity characteristic of him Lev Nikolayevich has recalled the case, endured once again all the feelings that agitate and disturb him at the thought of this evil deed, and put them down in the form of a letter to me with which I gladly complement my account in this chapter.[5]

Tolstoy's letter in its final form read as follows:

Dear friend Pavel Ivanovich!

I am very glad to fulfill your wish and tell you more fully what I thought and felt concerning the incident of my defense of the soldier about which you are writing in your book. That incident had much more influence on my life than all the seemingly more important events of life: the loss of or recovery of wealth, successes or failures in literature, even the loss of people close to me.

I shall tell how it happened and then try to express the thoughts and feelings that were roused in me by this event at the time and by my recollection of it now.

I do not remember what I was working on or absorbed in then—you will know better than I; I only know that at the time I was living a peaceful, self-satisfied, and thoroughly egotistical life. In the summer of 1866, Grisha Kolokoltsov, who as a cadet visited the Bers and was known to my wife, came to see us quite unexpectedly. It turned out he was serving in an infantry regiment stationed in our neighborhood. He was a merry, good-natured lad, especially occupied at the time with his small Cossack saddle horse, on which he liked to prance, and he often rode over to see us.

Thanks to him, we also met his regimental commander, Colonel Yunosha [the censor obscured the name by making it Colonel Yu——] and A. M. Stasyulevich, the brother of the well-known editor, who had been demoted to the ranks or sent for a soldier for some political affair (I do not remember which) and who was serving in the same regiment.

In his May 10 letter to Mikhail Stasyulevich, Tolstoy got Alexander's name wrong and otherwise indicated he did not know him well. "For my biography," he told Mikhail in part, "I have just described a certain case that is memorable to me and that brought me together with your late brother, Matvei Matveyevich, I believe. Following his degradation he was a junior officer in a regiment stationed near Yasnaya Polyana. I have very pleasant memories of him. He gave me the idea of defending a soldier of their regiment who was being court-martialed for striking his company commander. He did everything he could to save the soldier's life, but despite his effort and mine the soldier was executed. What kind of man was your brother? Why was he reduced to the ranks? Why did he die in such a strange way? If it is not difficult and not unpleasant for you, answer. This is not cold curiosity; as I am writing in my recollections, I had for him at the time a mixed feeling of sympathy, compassion, and respect."[6]

Stasyulevich was no longer a young man. He had only recently been promoted from soldier to ensign and joined the regiment of his former comrade Yunosha, now his superior officer. Both Yunosha and Stasyulevich rode over to see us occasionally. Yunosha was a stout, red-faced, good-natured man, still a bachelor, one of those men often met with in whom the quality of humanity is not evident because of the conventional posture in which they find themselves, the preservation of which they make their chief aim in life. For Colonel Yunosha that posture was the posture of a regimental commander. Judging from the human point of view, it is impossible to say of such a man whether he is good, whether he is reasonable, because one does not know what he would be like if he stopped being a colonel, a professor, a minister, a judge, or a journalist and stood forth as a man. So it was with Colonel Yunosha. He was an industrious regimental commander, a proper guest, but what kind of man he was it is impossible to say. I think he himself did not know and was not interested [in finding out]. Yet Stasyulevich as a man was alive, though disfigured in many ways, most of all by the misfortunes and humiliations that he, an ambitious and proud man, had painfully endured. So it seemed to me, but I did not know him sufficiently to go more deeply into the state of his soul. I know only that contact with him was pleasant and aroused a mixed feeling of compassion and respect.

Gusev wrote in his diary on May 1 that Tolstoy burst into tears while dictating this last sentence.[7]

Later on I lost sight of Stasyulevich, but not long after, when the regiment was stationed in another place, I found out that for no personal reasons, so they said, he took his own life and did so in the strangest way. Early one morning he put on a heavy quilted coat [in 1901 he had told Goldenweizer it was a raccoon coat] and walked into a river and, when he reached a deep place, he drowned because he could not swim. [In *Father Sergei* Tolstoy wrote that Sergei considered suicide by drowning but gave up the idea because he could swim.]

I do not remember whether it was Kolokoltsov or Stasyulevich who, having come to see us one day in summer, told us about an incident—most terrible and unusual for military men—that had occurred in their area: a soldier had struck a company commander, a captain, an academician [graduate of the General Staff Academy], in the face. Stasyulevich spoke with particular warmth and feeling about the fate of the soldier, who, according to Stasyulevich, expected the death penalty, and he asked me to be the soldier's counsel before the military court.

I should say that for some men to sentence others to death and for still other men to carry out the deed has not only always revolted me but seemed to me impossible, fabricated, one of those acts in the execution of which one refuses to believe although one knows they have been and are being carried out by men. The death penalty was and has remained for me one of those human acts the knowledge of whose execution does not intrude upon my awareness of the impossibility of its being carried out.

I understood before and continue to understand now that under the influence of temporary irritation, anger, revenge, or the loss of consciousness of his humaneness a man may kill defending someone close to him, even himself, that he may, under the influence of patriotic herd hypnosis, exposing himself to death, take part in collective murder in war. But that men in full possession of their human characteristics can calmly and deliberately admit the necessity of murdering a man like themselves and force other men to perform an act so contrary to human nature— that I never understood. And I did not understand it when

173

Tolstoy Breaks Silence

I was living my limited egotistical life in 1866, and that is why, strange as it may have been, I took on this business with hope of success.

I remember that having arrived at the village of Ozerki, where the accused was held (I do not quite remember whether it was in a special location or the one in which the act was committed) and entering a low brick *izba,* I was met by a short man with prominent cheekbones, more stout than lean, which is very rare among soldiers, with a simple, expressionless face. I do not remember whom I was with, Kolokoltsov it seems. When we entered, he rose and stood at attention. I explained to him that I wanted to be his counsel for the defense and asked him to tell me what had happened. He said little of his own accord and only in reply to my questions answered reluctantly: *"Tak tochno"* [precisely]. The purport of his answers was that he was bored and that his company commander was demanding. "He leaned on me a lot," he said.

The situation was as you have described it but [to say] that he drank to give himself courage is hardly fair.

As I understood the reason for his act, it was that the company commander, a man always outwardly calm, drove him to the last degree of exasperation, with his soft smooth voice demanding unquestioning obedience and the doing over again of work the scribe considered correctly done. The point of the matter, as I then understood it, was that besides the official relations between these men there was a very painful man-to-man relationship—an attitude of mutual hatred. As often happens, the company commander was antagonistic to the accused, a feeling that was reinforced by a suspicion the man hated him because he was a Pole, in response to which he hated his subordinate and, taking advantage of his position, took pleasure in always being dissatisfied with everything the scribe did and forced him to rewrite more than several times what the scribe considered to be irreproachably done. For his part the scribe hated the company commander both because he was a Pole and because he did not acknowledge his competence as a scribe and, above all, because of his calmness and the inaccessibility of his position. Finding no outlet, that hatred flared up more intensely with each new reproach, and when it reached its high point burst out in a way he himself did not anticipate. You say the explosion was provoked because the company commander said he would punish him with birch rods. That is not true. The company commander simply gave him back a paper and ordered him to correct it, to rewrite it.

On this point Tolstoy contradicted not only all other evidence available to Biryukov, but the implication of his own plea to the court, in which he said the captain "punished" Shabunin.

> The court soon convened. Yunosha was the president, Kolokoltsov and Stasyulevich the [other] two members. The accused was brought in. After I forget what formalities I read my plea . . .

Here, during the dictation of the first draft, according to Gusev, Tolstoy burst into tears for the second time after saying: "I read my feeble, miserable plea, which as I read it now I will not call strange but simply shameful. I pleaded the law, such and such articles, such and such a volume, when the plea concerned the life and death of a man."[8] He changed the wording sometime later on. He deleted the words *feeble* and *miserable* and altered what came after so that the final version read:

> . . . which as I read it now I will not call strange but simply shameful. The judges, concealing their boredom evidently for the sake of propriety, listened to all the banalities I uttered as I quoted such and such articles of such and such a volume, and when everything had been heard, they went out to confer. At that conference, as I later found out, only Stasyulevich favored the application of the stupid article I

cited, namely acquittal of the accused owing to acknowledgment of his being not answerable for his actions. But Kolokoltsov, a kind and good lad, though he truly wished to be agreeable to me, nevertheless submitted to Yunosha, and his vote decided the matter. The sentence of death by firing squad was read out. Immediately after the trial I wrote, as you say, a letter to one close to me and to the court [in St. Petersburg], the maid of honor Alexandra Andreyevna Tolstoy, asking her to appeal to the emperor —the emperor then was Alexander II—for a pardon on behalf of Shibunin [sic]. I wrote to Tolstoy [Alexandra] but absent-mindedly did not give the name of the regiment in which the incident occurred. She turned to the minister of war, Milyutin, but he said it was impossible to petition the emperor without designating the regiment of the accused. She so wrote me, and I hastened to reply, but the regimental command also hurried, and by the time there was no obstacle to presenting the petition to the emperor, the execution had taken place.

All the other details in your book, including the Christian attitude of the people to the executed one, are absolutely true.

Yes, it was terribly revolting to me now to·reread my pitiful, disgusting speech for the defense, which you have printed [evidently in galley form, because the book did not come out until September]. Speaking of the most obvious offense against the laws of God and man, which some men were preparing to commit against their brother, I did nothing better than cite some stupid words written by somebody else, called laws.

Yes, I am ashamed now to read this pitiful, stupid defense. You see, if only a man understands what people have gathered to do, sitting in their uniforms on three sides of a table and imagining that because they are so seated in their uniforms, because certain words are printed on various pages under headlines in various books, because of all this they can violate the eternal, common law, which is written not in books but in the hearts of all men,

then, you see, the one thing that can and must be said to
such people is to implore them to remember who they are
and what they propose to do. In no way should he cun-
ningly with false and stupid words called laws show that it
is possible not to kill the fellow. You see, to show that the
life of every man is sacred, that no man has the right to
deprive another of life—all men know this, and it cannot
be proved because it is not necessary to prove it. Only one
thing is possible and necessary and must be: to try to free
the judges of people from that stupefaction that leads them
toward such a wild and inhumane purpose. To prove this
is like proving to a man that he should not do what is
repulsive and contrary to his nature: that he should not go
naked in winter, that he should not feed on the contents of
dustbins, that he should not walk on all fours. That it is
repulsive and contrary to human nature was shown to men
long ago in the story of the woman who was about to be
stoned to death.

Is it possible that since that time men have emerged—
Colonel Yunosha and Grisha Kolokoltsov on his little horse
—who are so righteous they are no longer afraid to cast the
first stone?

I did not understand this then. I did not understand this
when through [Alexandra] Tolstoy I petitioned the emperor
for the pardon of Shibunin. I cannot but be amazed now at
the delusion I was in that everything that happened to
Shibunin was quite normal . . .

In Biryukov's published text there follows a gap, indicating
that the rest of this sentence and paragraph were deleted by
the censor. The censored lines are included here.

and that the participation, though indirect, in this affair of
the man they called emperor was also normal. And I *begged*
that man to pardon another, as if such a pardon were in
anyone's *power*. If I had been free from the universal stu-
por, I should have done one thing with respect to Alexan-

der II and Shibunin. I should have asked him not to pardon Shibunin but to pardon himself, that he get away from the terrible shameful position in which he found himself, involuntarily having a part in all crimes (according "to law"), because being in a position to stop them he did not stop them.

At the time I understood nothing about this. I only vaguely felt that something had happened that must not be, that cannot be, that this affair was not an accidental occurrence but in profound connection with all the errors and calamities of mankind, indeed that it lay at the root of all the errors and calamities of mankind.

Even then I vaguely felt that the death penalty, which is conscious, deliberate, premeditated murder, is directly contrary to the Christian law we ostensibly profess, a matter that manifestly infringes upon the possibility of a reasonable life and any morality whatsoever, because it is clear that if one man or group of men can decide it is necessary to kill one man or many, then there is no reason why another man or other men cannot find the same kind of necessity to kill other men. What kind of reasonable life or morality can there be among people who of their own will can murder one another? I vaguely felt even then that the justification of murder by the church and science, instead of achieving their goal—justification—on the contrary testifies to the falsity of the church and the falsity of science. I vaguely felt this for the first time in Paris when I witnessed from afar the death penalty; I felt it more clearly, much more clearly, when I took part in this affair. But I still feared to trust myself and divorce myself from the judgment of the whole world. I was brought only much later to the necessity of believing myself and to a denial of those two terrible frauds that hold the people of our time in their power and produce all those calamities from which mankind suffers: the falsity of the church and the falsity of science. [Tolstoy used the word *science* in the sense of a branch of knowledge or department of learning, specifically the law and interpretations of evolution.]

Guilt and Remorse

Only much later, when I began to examine attentively the arguments by which the church and science try to support and justify the existence of the state, did I see the obvious and flagrant frauds by which church and science hide from men the crimes committed by the state. In the catechism and scientific books distributed by the millions I saw the arguments by which the necessity and legality of the murder of some people at the will of others are explained.

Tolstoy now turned on the Orthodox catechism he had learned as a boy in the following lines, which were censored from Biryukov's chapter:

Thus, in connection with the sixth commandment—thou shalt not kill—men learn to kill in the very first lines of the catechism.

"QUESTION: What is forbidden in the sixth commandment?

"ANSWER: Murder or the taking of one's neighbor's life by any means.

"QUESTION: Is every taking of a life a transgression of the law; i.e., murder?

"ANSWER: It is not a transgression of the law, murder, when they take a life in the line of duty: for example, (1) when they punish a criminal according to law and (2) when they kill an enemy in war on behalf of the sovereign and the motherland."

And further:

"QUESTION: What instances could be regarded as a transgression of the law; i.e., murder?

"ANSWER: When someone conceals or liberates a murderer."

Following these censored lines, Tolstoy's letter continues.

In "scientific" works of two kinds—works called jurisprudence with their criminal *law* and works called purely scientific—the same thing is demonstrated with great narrow-mindedness and audacity. There is nothing to be said about criminal law; it is just a series of obvious sophistries, the aim of which is to justify all sorts of violence of man against man, even murder. In scientific works, beginning with Darwin, who puts the law of the struggle for existence at the foundation of life's progress, the same thing is implied. Some *enfants terribles* of this doctrine say it frankly, like the well-known professor of Jena University, Ernst Haeckel, in his celebrated work, the gospel for unbelievers, *The Natural History of Creation*:

(Haeckel was a German biologist and philosopher who developed a form of monism, based on Darwin's theories, which held that reality is an organic whole with no independent parts. Tolstoy heard of the paragraph he quotes here from his friend Yevgeni Popov, who also contributed to the Intermediary.)

"Artificial selection has exerted a highly favorable influence on the cultural life of mankind. How great in the complex movement of civilization is, for example, the influence of a good school education and upbringing. Like artificial selection the death penalty exerts a similarly beneficial influence, although at the present time many people speak warmly in support of the abolition of capital punishment as a 'liberal measure' and in the name of false humanitarianism produce a series of absurd arguments. In fact, however, capital punishment for the huge majority of incorrigible criminals and villains is not only just retribution for them but a great boon for the better part of mankind, just as for the successful cultivation of a well-tended garden the destruction of harmful weeds is required. And just as the painstaking removal of undergrowth brings more light, air, and space to field plants, the assiduous extermination of all inveterate criminals not only facilitates the 'struggle for existence' of the better part of mankind

180

but promotes artificial selection advantageous to it, because in that way the possibility of passing on their bad qualities will be taken from these degenerate dregs of mankind."

The words roused Tolstoy's indignation. He went on:

And people read that, teach it, call it science, and it enters no one's head to put the question that naturally presents itself, that if it is useful to kill bad people, who decides who is bad? I, for instance, consider I know no one worse or more harmful than Mr. Haeckel. But, really, am I and some others of my persuasion to sentence Mr. Haeckel to be hanged? On the contrary, the more profound the error of Mr. Haeckel, the more I wish him to come to reason, and in no case would I wish to deprive him of this possibility.

It is the lies of church and science such as these that have brought us to the position in which we find ourselves. Not months but years have passed during which there is not a day without executions and murders, and some people are pleased when there are more murders by the government than murders by revolutionaries, and others are pleased when more generals, landlords, merchants, and policemen are killed. On the one side, rewards of ten to twenty-five rubles for murder; on the other, revolutionaries honor murderers and exproprietors and extol them as heroes.

The censor cut the rest of this paragraph, which continued as follows:

They pay fifty rubles per execution to the voluntary executioner. I know the case of a man who went to the president of a court that had condemned five men to death with a request that the carrying out of the executions be turned over to him because he would do it cheaply: for fifteen rubles a man. I do not know whether the authorities accepted or rejected the proposition.

Tolstoy Breaks Silence

The uncensored part of the letter went on:

> Yes, fear not those who kill the body but those who kill the body and the soul.

Here the censor killed another line, one that Gusev says caused Tolstoy to burst into tears for the third time:[9]

> And they have killed and are killing the soul more and more.

Nearing the end, Tolstoy returned briefly if inexplicitly to the Shabunin affair:

> All this I understood much later but vaguely felt at the time I defended that unfortunate soldier so stupidly and shamefully. And that is why I say that case had a very strong and important influence on my life.
>
> Yes, that case had an enormous and most beneficial influence on me. On that occasion I felt for the first time: first, that all violence presupposes for its accomplishment murder or the threat of it, and that is why all violence is linked inescapably to murder; second, that a state system, which is unthinkable without murder, is incompatible with Christianity; and third, that what we call science is only the false justification of existing evil, as was church doctrine before it.
>
> This is clear to me now, but then there was only a vague consciousness of the falsehood amid which I was living.
>
> LEO TOLSTOY

Yasnaya Polyana
May 24, 1908[10]

In short, so Tolstoy implied, he defended Shabunin—and routinely, at that—because he opposed capital punishment and not because he cared about the soldier's life; he "understood" later on—"much later."

Guilt and Remorse

Understood what? That only the state and church and "science" were responsible for what happened in 1866? Or that he should have fought harder? That he should not have gone hunting the day after the execution or danced to the music of the band that had played on the field of death?

Tolstoy did not say. He revealed how he felt about his plea to the court. In his own dogmatic fashion he acknowledged the effect the entire episode had had on him. But he would go no further. He would not say whether he was present at the execution. He would not say how many months or years passed before he began to reflect on the affair. He would not tear down the wall that separated the holy of holies of his soul from other people.

Few men do. Still fewer men, I think, tell as much about their intimate past as Tolstoy told Biryukov and the world in this almost forgotten letter.

17

The Last Years

So far as I can tell, Biryukov's account of the affair aroused little public interest when his second volume came out in September 1908 (at the same time as Maude's first). The available record gives no indication that anyone denounced Tolstoy for his actions or attitude in 1866 or praised him for having the courage to tell as much as he told forty-two years after the event. It was as if his eminence as a writer and thinker, the adulation he excited among his followers, the hatred he stirred among men whose views he scorned, and the shield his family and friends held before him stifled discussion. As indicated earlier, his wife and children ignored the letter when they published their recollections; and in time Biryukov's second volume dropped from sight. A French translation appeared in Paris in 1909.[1] The Russian version was reprinted in Berlin in 1921.[2] Unlike his first volume, however, the second, evidently smothered in the marketplace by Maude's first, was not translated into English, and for many years Maude persisted in holding to his account of the affair or veiling Biryukov's. In his own second volume, which came out in 1910, Maude said that Biryukov's work had been "of great use to me," adding: "On several important matters our conclusions differ, but that in no way diminishes my obligation to him."[3] What "important matters"? The Shabunin affair may well have been one of them, because Maude hurried through the year 1908 without mentioning Tolstoy's letter, as in his earlier volume he had ignored Tolstoy's plea to the court. Furthermore, in *Family Views of Tolstoy*, which he published in 1926, Maude dropped Stasyulevich's name from the memoirs of Sonya's sister Tanya.[4] The time came, however, when in translating Tolstoy's works he had to deal with the case, and he did so in 1937 (after Biryukov's death and a year before his own). He began a translation with a bracketed paragraph in which he implied that the whole story was rather well known before Tolstoy wrote to Biryukov. It was not, as his own casual treatment of the case indicates. Said Maude: "[When dealing in his biography of L. N. Tolstoy with the incident of Tolstoy's defence of a soldier on trial for striking an officer, Biryukov asked Tolstoy to tell him something more than had been previously published about it, and Tolstoy wrote him the following letter.]"[5] Maude then omitted from the letter the paragraph in which Tolstoy wrote: "The situation was as you have described it but [to say] that he drank to give himself courage is hardly fair."[6] He also left out another paragraph in which Tolstoy referred to Biryukov's account: "All the other details in your book . . . are absolutely true."[7]

In sum, and for whatever reasons, Tolstoy's recollection and estimate of the affair passed virtually unnoticed—everywhere, one may believe, except in the higher echelons of church and state. The censored version was authorized, but state and church had no intention of letting it go at that. In 1909 the police raided Biryukov's house, banished Chertkov from Tula province, and exiled Gusev to a remote village in the Urals, from which he would not be allowed to return in Tolstoy's lifetime; and the old man fought back even as he continued to do battle with Sonya, who with determination to the point of frenzy struggled to gain possession of the rights to his works after death. But church and state were one thing, Sonya something else, and the day came when he could stand her no longer. About seven o'clock in the morning on October 28, 1910, accompanied by Dr. Makovitsky, he left home—for good—under cover of darkness, rather like Shabunin when he ran away from the Ekaterinoslav Life Grenadiers, "not knowing where to or what for." He told his daughter Alexandra, the only one of the children still living at home, to join him the next day at Optina Monastery, near Kozelsk; they would go on from there. For Sonya there was only a note to be given to her when she awoke:

> My departure will grieve you. I am sorry for that, but please understand and believe that I could not act otherwise. My position in the house is becoming and has become unbearable. Apart from anything else, I can no longer live in these conditions of luxury in which I have been living, and I am doing what old men of my age commonly do: leaving this worldly life in order to live out my last days in peace and solitude.
>
> Please try to understand this and do not follow me if you learn where I am. Your coming would only make your position and mine worse and would not alter my decision. I thank you for your honorable forty-eight years of life with me, and I beg you to forgive me for anything in which I have been at fault towards you, as I with all my soul forgive you for any wrong you have done to me. I advise you to reconcile yourself with the new position in which my departure places you and not to have an unkindly feeling towards me. If you want to report anything to me, give it to Sasha [their daughter Alexandra]. She will know where I am and will forward what is necessary. But she cannot tell you where I am, for she has promised me not to tell anyone.[8]

Reading the first line in the morning, Sonya shrieked and rushed toward the pond, intending to drown herself. She slipped, fell in, and was pulled out by Alexandra, Valentin

Bulgakov, who had taken Gusev's place as Tolstoy's secretary, and several servants. She tried to throw herself out of the window, again raced to the pond, was pulled back. Somewhat calmer the next day, she wrote a letter of her own:

> Lyovochka, darling, come home and save me, dear, from a second attempt at suicide. Lyovochka, friend of my whole life, I will do everything, everything you wish; I will renounce all luxury entirely; I'll be friendly with your friends; I'll cure myself; I'll be kind. Dear, dear, come back; you must save me. Even the Gospel says you can never, in *any circumstances*, desert your wife. My dear, darling, friend of my soul, save me, return. Come back if only to say farewell to me before we part forever.[9]

It was too late. Tolstoy's mind was set. At Optina Monastery on the twenty-ninth he dictated an article to Alexei Sergeyenko, Chertkov's secretary, who had arrived to assist him that morning. He called it *Really Effective Means*, and understandably it was against capital punishment. He concluded with these words: "For that reason if we really want to get rid of the error of the death sentence and, most important of all, if we are in possession of the knowledge that makes this error impossible, then let us spread this knowledge to others regardless of threats, deprivation, and suffering, for that is the only effective means of struggle."[10]

As things turned out, except for a few letters, this was the last thing he ever wrote.

Tolstoy drove on to Shamardino Convent to see his sister, Marya, who had been a nun there since 1890. Then, with Makovitsky and Alexandra, who had come as planned from Yasnaya Polyana, he boarded a train on the thirty-first for points south.

A sudden chill. Weakness. They took him off the train at Astapovo station. Chertkov and Goldenweizer were informed. Pneumonia set in. Alexandra wired her brother Sergei to bring a doctor from Moscow.

What about Sonya? Should they tell her? No. Tolstoy did not want to see her or his other children; their place, he thought, was with their mother. But Sonya heard where he was from a journalist and set off by special train with her daughter Tatyana and sons Ilya, Andrei, and Mikhail (Leo was in Paris). By the time she arrived, Sergei and Chertkov were already there. So was a priest, who had vain hopes of persuading Tolstoy to repent and receive the last sacrament of the church. So, too, were the police, to keep order and prevent a popular demonstration on his behalf or whatever they feared. Reporters hurried down from Moscow. As news of his plight spread, telephone calls and telegrams came in from all over the world.

Tolstoy was dying, and no one allowed Sonya to see him or dared tell him she was nearby. Days passed. He was dying hard.

What about Sonya now? As the light began to fade from his once glittering eyes, they let her in. Sonya entered hesitantly, knelt at his bedside, kissed his forehead, and murmured, "Forgive me. Forgive me."

But Tolstoy did not hear. He was unconscious and died at 6:05 on the morning of November 7, 1910, a worn-out fighter, eighty-two years old, but a fighter to the end, who never forgot entirely about the execution of a soldier in a field near his home.

And still one wonders what kind of man he really was—what kind of man wrote *War and Peace, Anna Karenina, Resurrection,* and so much else. A saint? Certainly not. He never thought he was. He knew better. Much better. A hypocritical crank? Only to those who feared his words or sneered at his vision of a better world.

I see him as a human being with human weaknesses, who tried to overcome them in the only way he knew how or was capable of; an aristocrat who was deceived in the Sha-bunin affair by aristocratic army officers and an aristocratic minister of war; an artist, horrified by violence, who foresaw disaster more clearly than most of his contemporaries and sought to warn them.

One may be convinced his vision was impractical. It probably was, and yet there is something glorious about a fight to the finish for a losing cause, and in this nuclear age it may be well to remember that since his death in the stationmaster's house at Astapovo, several hundred million—*million*—men, women, and children have been killed or crippled in war and revolution; that society, in spite of him, still hangs, shoots, gases, and poisons men to death, or executes them by electricity.

One of the greatest novelists who ever lived, he failed in the great crusade he embarked upon after *Anna Karenina.* But he tried.

Notes

Preface

1. Pavel Biryukov, *Lev Nikolayevich Tolstoi: Biografiya*, vol. 2, p. 81.
2. Aylmer Maude, *The Life of Tolstoy: First Fifty Years*, p. 811.
3. N. N. Gusev, *Dva goda s L. N. Tolstim, 1907–1908* [Two years with L. N. Tolstoy, 1907–1908], p. 145.
4. Henri Troyat, *Tolstoy*, p. 305.
5. Ernest J. Simmons, *Leo Tolstoy*, p. 278.

Author's Notes

1. *L. N. Tolstoi: Polnoye sobraniye sochineniy* [Complete works], 90 vols. in 78 plus index. This is the Jubilee Edition and will be identified hereafter as JE. The name is *Shibunin* in vol. 3, p. 312; vol. 34, p. 600; vol. 37, pp. 68–72, 421, 473–77; vol. 46, p. 443; vol. 48, p. 385; vol. 64, p. 247; vol. 78, pp. 130, 140; and vol. 89, p. 95. It is *Shebunin* in vol. 50, pp. 291, 258–259, and *Shabunin* in vol. 56, pp. 402, 490. The index volume uses only *Shibunin*.
2. N. N. Gusev, *Lev Nikolayevich Tolstoi: Materialy k biografii s 1855 po 1869 god* [Material for a biography from 1855 to 1869], p. 658 n.

1. Tolstoy for the Defense

1. *Reminiscences of Lev Tolstoi by His Contemporaries*, trans. Margaret Wettlin: Gorky, p. 417; Nemirovich-Danchenko, p. 353.
2. Nathan Haskell Dole, *The Life of Count Tolstoi*, pp. 116–17.
3. Troyat, *Tolstoy*, p. 175.

Notes

2. The Crime and the Punishment

1. Pavel Biryukov, *Lev Nikolayevich Tolstoi,* vol. 2, p. 81; Maude, *Life of Tolstoy: First Fifty Years,* p. 810; Troyat, *Tolstoy,* p. 288.
2. Biryukov, *Lev Nikolayevich Tolstoi,* vol. 2, p. 82.
3. I. M. Ippolitov, "Sudebnaya rech L. N. Tolstogo," *Pravo,* August 24, 1903, col. 2015.
4. A copy of the code in force at that time is on deposit in the Russian section of the Library of Congress.

3. First Talk with the Accused

1. *Reminiscences of Lev Tolstoi by His Contemporaries,* p. 181.
2. JE, vol. 46, pp. 193–95.
3. Biryukov, *Lev Nikolayevich Tolstoi,* vol. 2, pp. 96–97.
4. JE, vol. 7, p. 61.

4. Tolstoy before the Trial

1. Troyat, *Tolstoy,* p. 133.
2. Tatyana A. Kuzminskaya, *Tolstoy as I Knew Him,* p. 416.

5. Tolstoy's Plea to the Court

1. Gusev, *Lev Nikolayevich Tolstoi: Materialy k biografii s 1855 po 1869 god,* p. 661.
2. Troyat, *Tolstoy,* p. 361.
3. Leo Tolstoy, *War and Peace,* trans. Louise and Aylmer Maude, p. 805.
4. JE, vol. 37, p. 68.
5. Biryukov, *Lev Nikolayevich Tolstoi,* vol. 2, p. 81.
6. JE, vol. 37, pp. 473–77.
7. Kuzminskaya, *Tolstoy as I Knew Him,* p. 207.
8. Biryukov, *Lev Nikolayevich Tolstoi,* vol. 2, p. 98.
9. Alexander Goldenweizer, *Vblizi Tolstogo,* vol. 2, pp. 88–89.

6. The Anatomy of Power

1. JE, vol. 61, pp. 137–39.
2. Alexander Kornilov, *Modern Russian History,* vol. 2, p. 107.

3. Gusev, *Lev Nikolayevich Tolstoi, Materialy k biografii s 1855 po 1869 god*, p. 659. See also Gusev, *Letopis zhizni i tvorchestva Leva Nikolayevicha Tolstogo, 1828–1890* [Chronicle of the life and creative work of Lev Nikolayevich Tolstoi, 1828–1890], p. 325.

4. Sonya A. Tolstoy, *The Diary of Tolstoy's Wife, 1860–1891*, trans. Alexander Werth, pp. 146–47.

5. Ibid., pp. 147–48.

6. Ibid., p. 148.

7. Afanasi A. Shenshin (Fet), *Moi vospominaniya* [My recollections], pp. 93–94.

8. JE, vol. 61, p. 145.

9. Gusev, *Lev Nikolayevich Tolstoi: Materialy k biografii s 1855 po 1869 god*, p. 662; Ippolitov, "Sudebnaya rech L. N. Tolstogo," col. 2021; Biryukov, *Lev Nikolayevich Tolstoi, vol. 2, p. 93.*

10. Biryukov, *Lev Nikolayevich Tolstoi,* vol. 2, p. 93.

11. Ippolitov, "Sudebnaya rech L. N. Tolstogo," col. 2015.

7. Strange Behavior

1. Biryukov's and Gusev's primary source for the scene after the execution was Nikolai Ovsiannikov, a junker in the Sixty-fifth regiment in 1866, who visited Tolstoy in 1889. His work, which was not available to me, was published as an article in *Russkoye Obozreniye* [Russian Review], no. 11, 1896, and in book form as *Epizod iz zhizni L. N. Tolstogo* in 1912 (Moscow: Posrednika).

2. Sonya A. Tolstoy, *Diary,* pp. 148–49.

3. JE, vol. 83, p. 110.

4. Ibid., pp. 110–11.

5. Ibid., pp. 111–12.

6. JE, vol. 61, p. 139.

7. Ibid., p. 144.

8. Kuzminskaya, *Tolstoy as I Knew Him,* pp. 374–75.

9. Sonya A. Tolstoy, *Diary,* p. 150.

10. *War and Peace,* p. 1072.

8. Back to *War and Peace*

1. Gusev, *Letopis,* pp. 331–32.

2. Kuzminskaya, *Tolstoy as I Knew Him,* p. 368.

3. JE, vol. 78, pp. 139–40.

4. Kuzminskaya, *Tolstoy as I Knew Him,* p. 368.

Notes

5. The following quotations are from Louise and Aylmer Maude's translation of *War and Peace*.

6. Eugene Schuyler, *Selected Essays*.

9. The Spiritual Crisis

1. Stefan Zweig, *The Living Thoughts of Tolstoi*, p. 2.

2. Troyat, *Tolstoy*, p. 393.

3. Simmons, *Leo Tolstoy*, p. 315.

4. R. F. Christian, *Tolstoy's Letters*, vol. 1, pp. viii–ix.

5. The following quotations are from David Magarshack's translation of *Anna Karenina*.

6. Christian, *Tolstoy's Letters*, vol. 2, p. 283.

7. This and the following quotations are from Nathan Haskell Dole's translation of *My Confession*, as presented by Stefan Zweig in *The Living Thoughts of Tolstoi*.

8. Simmons, *Leo Tolstoy*, p. 326.

9. Troyat, *Tolstoy*, p. 415.

10. Nathan Haskell Dole, *The Life of Count Tolstoi*, p. 255.

11. *Encyclopaedia Britannica*, 14th ed., s.v. "Tolstoy, Leo (Lyev) Nikolayevich."

10. In Moral Combat

1. Christian, *Tolstoy's Letters*, vol. 2, p. 347.

2. Simmons, *Leo Tolstoy*, p. 332.

3. Christian, *Tolstoy's Letters*, vol. 1, p. 333.

4. Simmons, *Leo Tolstoy*, p. 323.

5. Christian, *Tolstoy's Letters*, vol. 1, p. 336.

6. Ibid., vol. 2, p. 338.

7. Ibid., p. 340.

8. *Tolstoi i Turgenev: Perepiska* (Moscow, 1928), p. 114, as quoted in Simmons, *Leo Tolstoy*, pp. 371–72.

9. Ilya Tolstoy, *Reminiscences of Tolstoy: By His Son Count Ilya Tolstoy*, p. 36.

10. Ibid., pp. 178–79.

11. JE, vol. 50, p. 64.

12. Ibid., p. 66.

13. JE, vol. 64, p. 247.

11. *Resurrection*

1. W. Somerset Maugham, *The World's Ten Greatest Novels*, p. 45.
2. Sonya A. Tolstoy, *Diary*, December 5, 1890.
3. This and the following quotations are from Vera Traill's translation of *Resurrection*.
4. JE, vol. 53, p. 232.
5. *Reminiscences of Lev Tolstoi by His Contemporaries*, p. 316.
6. Kuzminskaya, *Tolstoy as I Knew Him*, p. 353.
7. Alexandra Tolstoy, *A Life of My Father*, p. 99.
8. Christian, *Tolstoy's Letters*, vol. 2, p. 546.
9. *Tolstoy on Civil Disobedience and Non-violence*, p. 163.
10. Christian, *Tolstoy's Letters*, vol. 2, pp. 567–70.
11. Ibid., p. 573.

12. The Church Strikes Back

1. Troyat, *Tolstoy*, p. 674.
2. Goldenweizer, *Vblizi Tolstogo*, vol. 1, pp. 88–89.
3. Troyat, *Tolstoy*, p. 587; Simmons, *Leo Tolstoy*, p. 593.
4. Simmons, *Leo Tolstoy*, pp. 594–95.
5. Ibid., pp. 599–600.

13. The Bar Strikes Back

1. Biryukov, *Lev Nikolayevich Tolstoi*, vol. 1, p. 9.
2. Ibid., p. 11.
3. Ibid., p. 12.
4. Christian, *Tolstoy's Letters*, vol. 2, pp. 621–22.
5. Paul Birukoff, *Leo Tolstoy: His Life and Work*, vol. 1, p. xxv.
6. There is a copy of this issue in the *Pravo* files at the International Law School Library, Harvard University.

14. Enter Biryukov

1. Birukoff, *Leo Tolstoy*, vol. 1, p. xiii.
2. Christian, *Tolstoy's Letters*, vol. 2, pp. 608–13.
3. Troyat, *Tolstoy*, p. 611.
4. Birukoff, *Leo Tolstoy*, vol. 1, p. xvii.
5. Ibid.

Notes

15. The Telltale File

1. Gusev, *Lev Nikolayevich Tolstoi: Materialy k biografii s 1855 po 1869 god*, p. 661.
2. Christian, *Tolstoy's Letters*, vol. 2, p. 658.
3. Maude, *Life of Tolstoy: First Fifty Years*, p. 811.
4. Maude, *Life of Tolstoy: Later Years*, Preface.
5. JE, vol. 78, p. 77.
6. Christian, *Tolstoy's Letters*, vol. 2, p. 676.
7. JE, vol. 37, pp. 421–22.

16. Guilt and Remorse

1. JE, vol. 56, p. 116.
2. JE, vol. 89, pp. 94–95.
3. JE, vol. 78, p. 130.
4. Early in *I Cannot Be Silent* Tolstoy says he was driven to begin writing that day because he had read in a newspaper article that twenty peasants had been hanged. Before he finished, on May 31, he learned that only twelve had been hanged, and he corrected the mistake in a footnote.
5. Biryukov, *Lev Nikolayevich Tolstoi*, vol. 2, p. 93.
6. JE, vol. 78, pp. 139–40.
7. Gusev, *Dva goda*, p. 145.
8. Ibid.
9. Ibid., p. 145.
10. JE, vol 37, pp. 67–75. The censored lines appear on pp. 72, 73, and 75.

17. The Last Years

1. Birukov, *Léon Tolstoi: Vie et oeuvre*, vol. 3, pp. 90–111.
2. Biryukov, *L. N. Tolstoi*, 3d rev. ed.
3. Maude, *Life of Tolstoy: Later Years*, Preface.
4. He included Yunosha's and Kolkoltsov's names, however.
5. Aylmer Maude, *Recollections and Essays by Leo Tolstoy*, p. 56.
6. Ibid., p. 59.
7. Ibid., p. 61.
8. Simmons, *Leo Tolstoy*, pp. 761–62.
9. Ibid., p. 763.
10. *Reminiscences of Lev Tolstoi by His Contemporaries*, p. 255.

Bibliography

Collected Works

L. N. Tolstoi: Polnoye sobraniye sochineniy [Complete works]. 90 vols. in 78 plus index. Moscow and Leningrad: Gosudarstvennoye Izdatelstvo Literatury, 1928–58, index 1964.
Reminiscences of Lev Tolstoi by His Contemporaries. Trans. Margaret Wettlin. Moscow: Foreign Languages Publishing House, 196[1].

Books

Bers, Stepan A. *Recollections of Count Leo Tolstoy.* London: William Heinemann, 1893.
Biriukoff, Paul. *The Life of Tolstoy.* 3 vols. condensed into 1. London and New York: Cassell, 1911.
Birukoff, Paul. *Leo Tolstoy: His Life and Work.* Vol. 1 only, New York: Scribner, 1906.
Birukov, P. *Léon Tolstoi: Vie et oeuvre.* Vol. 3 (orig. vol. 2). Paris: Mercure de France, 1909.
Biryukov, Pavel. *Lev Nikolayevich Tolstoi: Biografiya.* 3 vols. Moscow: Posrednika, 1906–10.
———. *L. N. Tolstoi: Biografiya.* 3d rev. ed. Berlin: I. P. Ladyzhnikova, 1921.
Christian, R. F. *Tolstoy's "War and Peace": A Study.* London: Oxford University Press, 1962.
———. *Tolstoy's Letters.* 2 vols. New York: Scribner, 1978.
Curtiss, John Shelton. *The Russian Army under Nicholas I (1825–1855).* Durham, N.C.: Duke University Press, 1965.

Bibliography

Dole, Nathan Haskell. *The Life of Count Tolstoi.* New York: Scribner, 1929.

Goldenweizer, Alexander B. *Vblizi Tolstogo* [Near Tolstoy]. 2 vols. Moscow, 1922–23.

Gorky, Maxim. *Reminiscences of Tolstoy, Chekhov, and Andreyev.* London: Hogarth Press, 1934.

Graham, Stephen. *Tsar of Freedom: The Life and Reign of Alexander II.* New Haven: Yale University Press, 1935.

Gusev, Nikolai N. *Dva goda s L. N. Tolstim, 1907–1908* [Two years with Tolstoy, 1907–1908]. 2d ed. Moscow: Tolstovskogo Muzeya, 1928.

————. *Lev Nikolayevich Tolstoi: Materialy k biografii s 1855 po 1869 god* [Material for a biography from 1855 to 1869]. Moscow: Nauk, 1957.

————. *Lev Nikolayevich Tolstoi: Materialy k biografii s 1870 po 1881 god* [Material for a biography from 1870 to 1881]. Moscow: Nauk, 1958.

————. *Letopis zhizni i tvorchestva Leva Nikolayevicha Tolstogo, 1828–1890* [Chronicle of the life and creative work of Lev Nikolayevich Tolstoi, 1828–1890]. Moscow: Nauk, 1958.

————. *Letopis zhizni i tvorchestva Leva Nikolayevicha Tolstogo, 1891–1910* [Chronicle of the life and creative work of Lev Nikolayevich Tolstoi, 1891–1910). Moscow: Nauk, 1960.

Hall, Walter Phelps, and William Stearns Davis. *The Course of Europe since Waterloo.* 2d ed. New York: Appleton-Century, 1947.

Hare, Richard. *Portraits of Russian Personalities between Reform and Revolution.* London: Oxford University Press, 1959.

Kornilov, Alexander. *Modern Russian History.* 2 vols. New York: Alfred A. Knopf, 1924.

Kropotkin, P. *Ideals and Realities in Russian Literature.* New York: Alfred A. Knopf, 1919.

Kuzminskaya, Tatyana A. (Bers). *Tolstoy as I Knew Him: My Life at Home and at Yasnaya Polyana.* (Russian Translation Series of the American Council of Learned Societies, W. Chapin Huntington, Series Editor.) New York: Macmillan, 1948.

Leon, Derrick. *Tolstoy: His Life and Work.* London: Routledge, 1944.

Maude, Aylmer. *The Life of Tolstoy: First Fifty Years.* London: Constable, 1908.

————. *The Life of Tolstoy: Later Years.* London: Constable, 1910.

————. *Family Views of Tolstoy.* Selected by and trans. with Louise Maude. Boston: Houghton Mifflin, 1926.

————. *The Life of Tolstoy.* London: Oxford University Press, 1930.

Bibliography

————. *Recollections and Essays by Leo Tolstoy.* London: Oxford University Press, 1937.

Maugham, W. Somerset. *The World's Ten Greatest Novels.* New York: Fawcett, 1956.

Mirsky, Dmitri S. *A History of Russian Literature.* Ed. and abr. Francis J. Whitfield. New York: Knopf, 1949.

Mosse, W. E. *Alexander II and the Modernization of Russia.* New York: Collier, 1962.

Nazaroff, Alexander I. *The Constant Genius.* New York: Frederick A. Stokes, 1929.

Noyes, George Rapall. *Tolstoy.* New York: Duffield, 1918.

Polner, Tikhon. *Tolstoy and His Wife.* Trans. Nicholas Wreden. New York: W. W. Norton, 1945.

Redpath, Theodore, *Tolstoy.* London: Bowes & Bowes, 1960.

Rolland, Romain. *Tolstoy.* Trans. Bernard Miall. New York: Dutton, 1911.

Schuyler, Eugene. *Selected Essays.* London: Samson Low, Marston, 1901.

Shenshin, Afanasi A. (Fet). *Moi vospominaniya, 1848–1889* [My recollections, 1848–1889]. 2 vols. Moscow, 1890.

Simmons, Ernest J. *Leo Tolstoy.* Boston: Little, Brown, 1946.

Spence, Gordon William. *Tolstoy the Ascetic.* New York: Barnes & Noble, 1968.

Steiner, Edward A. *Tolstoy: The Man and His Message.* New York: Fleming H. Revell, 1908.

Tolstoy, Alexandra L. *The Tragedy of Tolstoy.* Trans. Elena Varneck. New Haven: Yale University Press, 1933.

————. *A Life of My Father.* Trans. Elizabeth Hapgood Reynolds. New York: Harper, 1953.

Tolstoy, Ilya L. *Reminiscences of Tolstoy: By His Son Count Ilya Tolstoy.* Trans. George Calderon. New York: Century, 1914.

Tolstoy, Leo. *War and Peace.* Trans. Louise and Aylmer Maude, with a foreword by Clifton Fadiman. New York: Simon & Schuster, 1942.

————. *Anna Karenina.* Trans. and with a foreword by David Magarshack. New York: New American Library, 1961.

————. *Resurrection.* Trans. Vera Traill, with a foreword by Alan Hodge. New York: New American Library, 1961.

————. *Tolstoy on Civil Disobedience and Non-violence.* New York: New American Library, 1968.

Tolstoy, Leo L. *The Truth about My Father.* London: J. Murray, 1924.

Bibliography

Tolstoy, Sergei L. *Tolstoy Remembered by His Son Sergei Tolstoy.* Trans. Moura Budberg. New York: Atheneum, 1962.

Tolstoy, Sonya A. *The Diary of Tolstoy's Wife, 1860–1891.* Trans. Alexander Werth. London: Gollancz, 1928.

Tolstoy (Sukhotin), Tatyana L. *The Tolstoy Home.* New York: Columbia University Press, 1951.

———. *Tolstoy Remembered.* Trans. Derek Coltman. New York: McGraw-Hill, 1978.

Troyat, Henri. *Tolstoy.* Trans. Nancy Amphoux. Garden City, N. Y.: Doubleday, 1967.

Zweig, Stefan. *The Living Thoughts of Tolstoi.* London: Cassell, 1939.

Index

Index

Index

Index

Index

The Shabunin Affair

Designed by Richard E. Rosenbaum.
Composed by Eastern Graphics
in 10 point Linotron 202 Palatino, 3 points leaded,
with display lines in Palatino.
Printed offset by Vail-Ballou Press, Inc.
Bound by Vail-Ballou
in Joanna book cloth.

Library of Congress Cataloging in Publication Data

Kerr, Walter Boardman, 1911–
    The Shabunin affair.

    Bibliography: p.
    Includes index.
    1. Shabunin, Vasili. 2. Trials (Military offenses)—Soviet Union. 3. Tolstoy,
Leo, graf, 1828–1910. I. Title.
Law   343.47'0143   81-70715
    ISBN 0-8014-1461-X   344.703143   AACR2